Diversity
incorporated

'Managing Diversity is not easy to put into practice. In *Diversity Incorporated*, Johnson and Redmond have produced a book dealing with a great range of issues in an insightful and well-informed way. With such a comprehensive guide available, there can be no excuse now for organizations to claim "they didn't know".' – **Meredith Belbin**, *BelBin Associates.*

'Fairness at work and equality of opportunity are values about which we should all care. In recommending this book on managing diversity by Dr Ron Johnson and David Redmond, I do so confident in the knowledge that the guidance from its pages will serve as a pathway to new standards in diversity.' – **Bill Morris**, *General Secretary, T & G (Transport and General Workers Union).*

'The support we give to all our people arises from a very real commitment to provide an effective service in a diverse society, and Cleveland Police was honoured to be named as the most supportive employer of the year (in 2000) by the National Mentoring Consortium. I recommend this book as it deals with both the strategy and the practical steps that top people in organizations can take to achieve success through diversity management.' – **Barry Shaw**, *Chief Constable, Cleveland Police.*

'In our drive to maintain and improve the service to our customers, I recognise the business value of diversity management as described fully and in a stimulating way in this new book by Ron Johnson and David Redmond.' – **Martin Gwynn**, *Managing Director, BOC Distribution Services.*

'As a management team, we can identify with the practical advice provided in the new book by Ron Johnson and David Redmond. We fully appreciate the need to manage diversity and for years we have worked closely with the trade union in achieving this end.' – **Peter Fitzpatrick**, *Operations Director, Ciro Citterio.*

'I firmly believe this book gives an insight into the practical steps of managing diversity and ensuring that in any multi-cultural environment – providing there is a common goal and expectation – mountains can be climbed.' – **Ken Keir**, *Managing Director, Honda UK.*

Diversity
incorporated

▶ Managing people for success in a diverse world

Ron Johnson
David Redmond

London ● New York ● San Francisco ● Toronto ● Sydney ● Tokyo ● Singapore
Hong Kong ● Cape Town ● Madrid ● Paris ● Milan ● Munich ● Amsterdam

PEARSON EDUCATION LIMITED

Head Office
Edinburgh Gate
Harlow CM20 2JE
Tel: +44 (0)1279 623623
Fax: +44 (0)1279 431059

London Office:
128 Long Acre, London WC2E 9AN
Tel: +44 (0)20 7447 2000
Fax: +44 (0)20 7240 5771
Website:www.business-minds.com

First published in Great Britain in 2000

© Pearson Education Limited 2000

The right of Ron Johnson and David Redmond to be
identified as authors of this work has been asserted by them in
accordance with the Copyright, Designs and Patents Act 1988.

ISBN 0 273 65047 5

British Library Cataloguing in Publication Data
A CIP catalogue record for this book can be obtained from the British Library.

10 9 8 7 6 5 4 3 2 1

Typeset by Northern Phototypesetting Co Ltd, Bolton
Printed and bound in Great Britain by Biddles Ltd, Guildford & King's Lynn

The Publishers' policy is to use paper manufactured from sustainable forests.

Contents

Contents

About the authors

Ron Johnson, an independent consultant since 1980, specializes in corporate strategy and the management of change. He has been director of training at the Manpower Services Commission and twice vice-president (T&D) of the Institute of Personnel Management. Over recent years his main clients have been a selection of well-known plcs including BICC, Cadbury and British Airways. Much of his work has been concerned with helping organizations to involve people in all areas and at all levels. Ron has an interest in business planning and financial management. He is the author of a number of books on managing people, teamwork and business planning. In recent years he has taken a particular interest in assisting organizations to introduce team working throughout entire operational units. Much of his consultancy work in Europe has involved working in multinational teams and his UK teamwork development has often involved people of diverse backgrounds.

David Redmond, an independent consultant since 1990, has conducted a number of consultancy assignments concerned with employee relations, training, management development and quality programmes. David's extensive career in human resource management in the UK and overseas culminated in his appointment as director of human resources in BOC Distribution Services, a major distribution company serving Marks & Spencer, Sainsbury, Safeway and Tesco. During his 20 years with BOC Distribution Services David pioneered many developments in employee communications and participation. He took part in a number of employee involvement initiatives with the Institute of Personnel Development and the Involvement and Participation Association. David has worked closely with trade unions in developing these initiatives.

Ron Johnson and David Redmond are the joint authors of *The Art of Empowerment – the profit and pain of employee involvement* published by Pitman in 1997.

Foreword

We now operate in an international multicultural business environment which will progressively become more and more immediate as technology advances. The notion that 'diversity' in any guise within an organization should be considered a negative can only become a major stumbling block to the performance of the operation and therefore the wellbeing of the people employed in it. The reality is that diversity can be harnessed to become a massive positive.

I met Ron Johnson and David Redmond for a discussion regarding this book and I found our conversation very stimulating, not least because there was an immediate common understanding between the academic principles and the practical management processes in a successful company.

Diversity of national cultures creates a huge stimulation and at times some tension that results in initiatives leading to great performance. However, any organization can only operate with clarity if the core philosophy, management principles and work practices are accepted and become part of the individual and collective team's way of business life.

Honda was created 50 years ago as a motorcycle company and now sells 11 million products globally on an annual basis through multiplicity of product – cars, motor cycles and power equipment. The core of the great success of this time has been Soichiro Honda's philosophy applied at the creation of the business. He said that:

'Action without philosophy is a lethal weapon, philosophy without action is worthless.'

Any core corporate philosophy must be the fundamental key driver: it creates a common vision, value, commitment and focus; it helps us maintain a sense of uniqueness; and it also creates a business ethic and permanent targets.

The fundamental belief of the Honda way is respect for the individual, and this includes attention to initiative, equality and trust. Associates at Honda should not be bound by pre-conceived ideas but should think creatively and act on their own initiative and judgement while understanding that they must take responsibility for the results of those actions.

Equality means recognising and respecting individual differences in one another and treating each other fairly. Our company is committed to this principle and to creating equal opportunities for each individual. An individual's race, age, sex, religion, national origin, educational background and social or economic status have no bearing on his or her opportunities.

The relationship among Associates at Honda should be based on mutual trust. Trust is created by recognising each other as individuals, helping out where others are deficient, accepting help where we are deficient, sharing our knowledge and making a sincere effort to fulfil our responsibilities. This respect for the individual obviously defines our relationship with our customers, our business associates and of course members of society.

You create the catalyst for the principle of respecting the individual through the principle of the three joys – the joy of buying, the joy of selling and the joy of producing. In that regard our main concern comes back always to people, whether it be achieving satisfaction, exceeding expectations or creating genuine relationships. I firmly believe this book gives an insight into the practical steps of managing diversity and ensuring that in any multicultural environment – providing there is a common goal and expectation – mountains can be climbed.

Ken Keir
Managing Director, Honda UK

Acknowledgements

We are grateful to the following people who have been prepared to discuss the topic with us and to give us the benefit of their experience. In many cases these individuals have also provided valuable written material related to their organizations: Kay Allen (Diversity Manager, B&Q plc), Christine Bailey (Human Resources Director, Two Shires Ambulance NHS Trust), Meredith Belbin (BelBin Associates, Cambridge), Peter Buckingham (Director of Remuneration and Benefits, Reuters), Sue Cox (Group Personnel Director, Schroders plc), Professor John Fyfe, Mike Galloway (Principal, York College) and Julie Kitching (Personnel Adviser, York College), Paul Holt (Human Resources Director, BICC General), Paul Hughes (Head of Human Resources, Cleveland Police Force), Stella Jackson (formerly Head of Management Development, London Borough of Lewisham), Ana Paula Laissy (Head of the Non-Discrimination and Equal Opportunities Unit, European Commission, Brussels), Phillip Mansley (Foreign and Commonwealth Office), Terry Morgan (Human Resources Director, BAE Systems) and Richard Barr (Personnel Manager, Engineering, BAE Systems), Bill Morris (General Secretary, Transport and General Workers' Union, UK), Barry Camfield (Assistant General Secretary, Transport and General Workers' Union, UK) and Stella Guy (Regional Secretary, Transport and General Workers' Union, UK), Louise Redmond (Human Resource Director, Discovery, SmithKline Beecham), Fernand Sauer (Executive Director, The European Agency for the Evaluation of Medicinal Products) and Marino Riva (Head of Administration, The European Agency for the Evaluation of Medicinal Products), Paul Summerland (Human Resources Manager, Ciro Cittario), Les Shaw (Human Resources Director, Hickson & Welch Ltd), Jill Sheddon (Human Resources Director, Group Operations and Policies, Centrica plc), David Slingo (Human Resources Policy Manager, British Telecommunications plc), Madeleine Starr (Project Manager, Carers and Employment, Carers National Association, UK). We are particularly indebted to Ken Keir (Managing Director, Honda UK), not only for very helpful discussions and the information he provided, but also for contributing the Foreword.

Preface

For most organizations, the business case for managing diversity is compelling. The moral imperatives are weighty. But if you are serious about managing diversity you must first be prepared to face up to your own prejudice – and that of your senior colleagues. All of us look at other people through filters created by our experiences. The major problem in managing diversity is not the mechanics of policies and procedures. It is helping people to see each other afresh and to respect others who are different.

If we, and those who work with us, can reach that point, then the policies and procedures will work. Otherwise there will always be elements of discrimination, perhaps racism, sexism or homophobia. Individuals will be undervalued, underdeveloped, underused, and probably harassed as well. Managing diversity is not an issue only for the workplace. When you go home, to your family, your golf club or your local restaurant, you should value people and abhor discrimination there, too.

We assume that you are complying with the relevant legislation in this field. Beyond this, if you are honest, you will recognize that making special efforts may not dramatically further your organization's goals in the short run. But in the long run there are very real benefits from managing diversity: some organizations will gain more than others.

Two white men living in England have written this book, but we have endeavoured to give the text an international dimension based on our varied experiences here and overseas. These insights have been enhanced by many hours of discussion with friends and business associates who have worked in other countries, and/or who work within multinational companies where the need to promote diversity on a worldwide basis is a major factor. None of the senior people we interviewed considered that their organizations had 'arrived'. Diversity is a developing theme and organizations are at all different stages of development. Some are well ahead – but some are very far behind. We have also combed the literature for gems of insight and practical ideas.

We do not aim to present a formula, or to give detailed instructions, but rather to provide for the thoughtful senior executive the tools he or she needs to make strategic decisions about the management of diversity and to monitor the work of others engaged in the detailed tasks of implementation.

We have used the masculine and the feminine gender indiscriminately except where we are writing about specific individuals or dealing with gender-specific issues. The incidents noted are all based on real events, but in some cases we have omitted individual names and organizations, as we feel it might embarrass the people concerned if they could be identified.

1

The approach to diversity

▶ Managing diversity is not an option but a necessity

▶ Be honest

▶ The baseline is to comply with the law

▶ The business approach maximizes the asset of a diverse labour force

▶ Take into account the whole pool of labour and your customers

▶ Take a fresh look at people

▶ Learn to operate effectively in a global, diverse marketplace

▶ Consider the scope of 'disadvantage'

Organizations that seriously tackle diversity issues find that there are very real and tangible benefits that impact directly on the bottom line (*see* Chapter 2). In the modern world, people diversity is a fact of life.

Why manage diversity?

In many parts of the world people are no longer willing to be treated unfairly because they are women, or because they have some other distinguishing feature – be it race, nationality, creed, background, personality, sexual orientation, lifestyle, age or disability. Society expects organizations to treat people with respect and fairness, although in some regions this sense of fairness is less pronounced.

In many countries, notably Australia, Europe, Singapore, South Africa and the United States, these expectations have led to legislation. This may cover equality of opportunity in relation to gender, race, disability and age. It is therefore essential for organizations to be aware of the relevant law in each country, and to ensure that all employees adhere to it. Laws establish a baseline for the management of diversity. Some organizations may consider that this is enough.

There are two problems with this minimalist approach. The rules are changing. In many countries the legislation is gradually being extended. Furthermore, this limited view ignores the fact that a workforce made up of a diversity of people can, and should, become a positive asset – if the workforce is sensitively managed.

In Europe and America the need to consider the management of diversity arises in large part from **changes in the marketplace and in the workforce**. Over recent years we have seen the following features in the marketplace:

● more women at work

● more national, racial and cultural diversity in the workforce

● an increase in the average age of the workforce

● more companies that trade across national boundaries

● more multinational companies

● more use of digital technology in communications and trade.

There are other reasons to consider the desirability of recruiting and managing effectively a diverse workforce. Organizations that are located in and serve **multi-ethnic communities** find that it makes sense to seek to recruit their people from a cross-section of these populations. Examples include retailers, local authorities, health authorities and police forces. It means that within the organization there are people who appreciate the needs and aspirations of the population. If these employees are enabled and encouraged to make their contribution to the way the organization operates, a better service results. As customers recognize this, they respond positively and gain confidence in the organization.

Organizations that seek to recruit from the whole population generally find that **the pool of applicants is richer**. The basic skills of the workforce can be enhanced. Organizations that operate globally have come to recognize that talent is by no means restricted to prime-age Caucasian males! Such organizations recruit the best people wherever they come from and whatever the gender or race. The same principle applies to organizations that mainly employ people who work nearby.

Be honest

In setting out to manage diversity you will encounter two basic problems. The first is the potential conflict between your organization's goals and the cost of implementing change. The second is your prejudice and that of your senior colleagues. If you are not prepared to face these two problems honestly, the progress you make hereafter will be patchy and you will experience setbacks that people will find difficult to understand.

> ▶ Directors must face the prejudices that we each develop during our upbringing

Directors and senior managers must face the prejudices that we each develop during our upbringing. The extent to which we are prejudiced against people of another country, another race, another religion or whatever depends very much on social conditioning. This is very difficult to recognise at times, and even when we have recognized it, it is difficult to handle.

In some cultures a disabled person is regarded as a pariah, someone to keep away from in case they contaminate others. In 'western' culture there is a tendency to treat disabled people like children. The classic gaffe of asking the helper of a man in a wheelchair 'does he take sugar?' instead of asking the man himself is too near the truth for comfort.

Before you get down to any detailed analysis of your organization, think through how you personally see the situation. Talk to a few senior colleagues. How do you rate your organization and how much change do you think is really needed? Rate the organization on the following scale:

Model employer   We are a model employer, recruiting and promoting without discrimination and giving every employee an opportunity to develop his or her talents to the full. All our employees are wholeheartedly committed to this policy and approach.

Getting there   We have put in place policies and programmes that we believe will ensure that we recruit and promote people without discrimination and provide every

	employee with the opportunity to develop to the full. We have not yet secured the commitment of all our people to this policy.
Made a start	We are developing policies and programmes that we believe will ensure that we recruit and promote people without discrimination and provide every employee with the opportunity to develop to the full. Our management team is not fully convinced and we are working on that now.
Problem	We have a specific problem area concerning diversity that we need to address.
In the backwoods	I am reading this book in case there is anything I need to do. I think my organization has no problem. We have few women or ethnic minority people and they do not make any trouble. We have one or two disabled people where we can fit them in without too much trouble.

How you proceed will depend on the way you and your senior colleagues perceive your organization. If you see it as already making good progress, use the checklists in the book to make sure you are covering all the bases. If you are making a start or have a specific problem, you will need to tackle the following sections and Chapter 3 in a systematic way.

You must face up to the fact that if you propose to make any significant culture change this will involve cost in terms of senior management time and frustration, as well as money.

A fresh look at people

Take a fresh look at the whole question of managing people. Managing diversity is much more than equality of opportunities for women and race relations, although it includes these. Managing diversity today means considering individual people, and working out how to ensure that they are treated fairly, valued and provided with opportunities for development and progression.

It involves seeking out and removing the obstacles that individuals face as they look for advancement – whether this is related to gender, race,

creed, background, personality, sexual orientation, lifestyle, age or disability. A progressive policy also looks at other issues, such as employees responsible for caring for children or for sick or elderly relatives. It will also ensure that people are not disadvantaged because of their accent or where they live.

A few years ago there was a town in the North of England where unemployment in certain areas had persisted for very long periods. In one particular area there were whole streets where families had been unemployed for generations. No member of the family, parents, children or grandchildren, had ever been in paid employment. There were rumours – never substantiated to our knowledge – that when an employer saw an application with a postcode from this area it was binned immediately. That was the perception of many residents. It took great courage on the part of individuals to break out of this cycle of deprivation.

This requires a culture, led from the top, where every individual in the organization is valued and respected. This respect must be extended to the diversity of people in other organizations, particularly business contacts. Serious effort is needed to promote teamwork between people of different cultures, attitudes, values and aspirations.

Operating in the modern global economy means that many employers now have to learn to deal with people of different nationalities and cultures within their own organizations. Many more have to deal with overseas people on a regular basis. Thus senior management has to lead organizations where people diversity is a fact of life, and the skill required becomes an essential part of the manager's competence portfolio.

▶ **People diversity is a fact of life**

The internet has transformed international trade. The genie is out of the bottle and the business world will never be the same again. Even the smallest firms can trade globally and as a result, many of the prejudices of the past must be swept away. This compels us to review our attitudes to people who are different to ourselves, and whose values and ways of working we may find difficult to understand. It also makes new demands on people who work for us.

Directors and senior managers now recognize the crucial importance of a competent and committed workforce. The key to achieving this is (a) to create a supportive climate, and (b) to implement appropriate policies and procedures for recruitment and selection, and for the involvement, development and deployment of people. Increasingly, particular attention has to be paid to the diverse nature of the people you employ, the labour market from which employees are drawn and the customers they serve.

> ▶ **The new paradigm is to consider every person as an important individual**

Senior people must move beyond the point of thinking of people as mere members of this group or that – men, women, Asians, disabled or old. The **new paradigm is to consider every person** in the organization as an important individual, worthy of respect, fair treatment and the opportunity to develop and to contribute. Business gains arise from developing and using the potential of all the employees in the business and ensuring that the workforce is recruited from the widest possible population of appropriate job seekers.

Policies and procedures

To bring about change you must deal with the 'rules of behaviour' to which people are expected to adhere, and the attitudes they bring to the workplace. There are a number of key policies and procedures that your organization must address if the management of diversity is to make a full and positive impact on business success, in particular:

● recruitment

● disability

● induction and initial training

● selection

● appraisals

● reward systems

● discrimination

● harassment and bullying

● discipline and grievance

● language and culture

● information systems.

These topics will be covered in depth elsewhere. In developing these policies and procedures it is important to recognize the need to think beyond the 'disadvantaged groups'. A black 20-year-old girl with only one arm falls into three distinct disadvantaged groups in some societies. But if the young lady has a degree, a secure job where she is treated well, free from harassment, and given the opportunity to contribute to the organization, the fact that she is in these disadvantaged groups is not the point at issue. It becomes an issue if she is personally disadvantaged or mistreated in some way – whether or not that is related to gender, race or disability.

The positive approach is to promote a culture where every person counts, and every individual is accorded respect and fair treatment in the organization. This applies to the potential employees at the recruitment stage, as well as to employees in post. It also applies to the way people in your organization treat the people outside with whom they come into contact. These external contacts may be customers or suppliers.

Your organization should not only treat such people with respect, it should expect external people to treat your employees with respect as well. This can and should be written into your operating policies. You should not hesitate to take action if someone who is a customer or supplier, or who works for them, deals disrespectfully with a member of your staff. Organizations whose staff interact with individual customers at a personal level (for example, retailers, public transport, accident and emergency units) may have particular problems in protecting their staff from harassment, abuse or physical assault.

> **The fundamental aim is to integrate diversity into the way the organization operates**

The fundamental aim is to integrate diversity policies and procedures into the way the organization operates, not to impose a set of 'extra' demands. Apart from the introduction of policies and procedures, the organization's culture will probably need to change. The management of such a culture change has been covered in some depth in *The Art of Empowerment* (Johnson and Redmond, 1997) and will not be repeated in detail here.

In managing change, care is needed in identifying the parameters to be monitored, and the methods to be used. It is common practice to monitor such workforce features as age (but not in the USA) and gender, and sometimes race, nationality and disability. Monitoring staff with disabilities is often difficult because a person with a disability may not wish to be reminded of this fact or recorded on a file if she is working successfully in a job. Some organizations have found that labour turnover data by region or unit, coupled with exit interviews have shed light on possible areas for action.

The human resources director of a large multinational company noticed that in one overseas unit the labour turnover had risen substantially over a period of months. An initial investigation revealed that people were leaving because of the way they were treated by the boss. A deeper investigation revealed that some of these employees had become aware that the boss was swindling the firm. They felt uncomfortable and unable to report the matter. Rather than risk being implicated, they preferred to tender their resignations. When this was discovered, the allegation was investigated and the fraud verified. Once the company had sacked the boss and appointed a new person to take over, the labour turnover returned to a more reasonable level for that part of the world. The company reviewed its procedures for enabling individuals to report difficulties of this nature.

The disadvantaged

Many women who want to work face real problems in many societies. In many 'western' countries, considerable progress has been made in promoting equal opportunities for both sexes. Jobs traditionally reserved for men – or in some cases for women – have over the years been opened up to both sexes. Nevertheless, many anomalies remain. The key is to ensure that both men and women, managers and the managed, recognize the need to make decisions about recruitment, assessment, selection and development of people according to ability and potential, irrespective of gender.

People may be disadvantaged because of their nationality, race or even accent. This discrimination is not restricted to colour, and it is not particularly a 'white man's' problem. Prejudice is just as likely to come from a black person, or to exist between people of the same skin colour. All that is required is some way to differentiate an individual as being 'different'.

The plight of Moroccans in Paris, Turks in Berlin and in earlier times the Jamaicans in London and Negroes in Washington typifies the problems that minorities may face, particularly when large numbers descend on a metropolis. Governments may help, but employers have a key responsibility too, especially if they are major employers in a locality. Sectarian prejudice is another potential problem. Employers will need to take account of religious holy days, be they Christian, Buddhist, Moslem or whatever. Account may have to be taken of specific garments with religious or cultural significance, for example the Sikh's turban. Cultural differences are often more subtle, but provide emotive areas for misunderstanding (*see* Chapter 13).

Language poses another type of problem. Now that the use of English (albeit often in its American form) is widespread, many international companies tend to operate mainly in that language. This is particularly true of organizations in the finance sector and pharmaceuticals. But even these organizations have to translate their product literature into the local languages to communicate with their customers, and many of their employees will not be bilingual. Language and culture must be taken into account very carefully at all stages in employment policies and procedures, especially in selection tests.

In some cultures older people are respected and their views and efforts valued. In other societies, people are considered 'past it' when they reach the ripe old age of 40. In many western societies a fall in the birth rate and increased longevity is shifting the age profile of the population – and of the workforce. More older people are seeking work, and moreover people with valuable skills. In many countries the need to respect older people and to offer them employment without discrimination on the basis of age is gaining ground. Thpe USA has decided to enshrine in law the right of older people to be treated fairly and employers have accommodated this requirement.

> ▶ **The disadvantage that a person with a disability faces depends on the form of disablement**

The disadvantage that a person with a disability faces depends on the form of disablement. Some disabilities we can observe, for example blindness or paraplegia, and to some extent the measures that can be taken to help are comparatively straightforward. Other forms of disablement require more thought. Partially sighted people, people who walk with difficulty and deaf people find that all too often life is made difficult when it is not really necessary.

Discrimination on the grounds of sexual orientation still persists in many employment situations. This is a subject that has already been brought into the legal arena and it must be carefully considered in the determination of organizational policies and practices. Already several major organizations have taken account of single-gender partnerships in their 'family-friendly' policies.

The problem of balancing working life with life apart from work is a key issue. The problems that mothers face has been discussed at length, but nevertheless they are very real and no employer worth his salt will ignore them. The problems of mothers at work need to be considered on an individual basis. All mothers are not the same; they have different backgrounds, different levels of support, different incomes and different approaches to the upbringing of their offspring. Many modern men take an active part in the upbringing of their children, undertaking every activity from changing diapers to reading the bedtime story.

But parents are not the only carers. Many workers are also responsible for the care of disabled relatives. As the population ages in many countries, workers find themselves caring for elderly relatives. Some people are locked into caring so firmly that they find it difficult to get out to work at all, even on a part-time basis. Such carers could be considered as another disadvantaged group, but once again it would be wrong to think in those terms. Each carer has individual circumstances that need to be taken into account.

Progress checklist

☑ Have you considered carefully the need to manage diversity?

☑ Have you and your senior people honestly faced up to your prejudices and the potential conflict between your organization's goals and a costly change programme?

☑ Do you have an effective mechanism to ensure that all your employees adhere to the law in relation to equality of opportunity and freedom from harassment?

☑ Have you considered the effect of diversity in the workforce and in your customer base?

☑ Have you considered the advantages of recruiting from a diverse workforce?

☑ Have you achieved a culture that welcomes diversity and derives positive gains from a diverse workforce?

☑ Are you confident that your policies and practices support the effective management of a diverse workforce?

[?] Do your information management systems support the empowerment of all your people?

[?] Do your policies and practices take into account the wide variety of disadvantages that people face in their working lives?

2

Benefits and pitfalls

▶ Reap both tangible and intangible benefits from effective diversity management

▶ Adherence to legal requirements forms a baseline for action

▶ Minimize labour costs by sound diversity management

▶ Manage diversity to succeed in a diversely populated business environment

▶ Respond positively to the pressures of society

▶ Manage multicultural teams and create a winning workforce

▶ Avoid the inevitable pitfalls

Organizations that seek actively to manage diversity find that there are very real and tangible gains. You can manage diversity to improve the effectiveness of your organization, to recruit from the widest pool of talent, and to enable the people you employ to contribute fully to the organization's goals. Virtually every organization operates within a multidimensional 'people' environment, either in terms of the customers it serves or the labour force from which its workforce is recruited. More often both the customers and the employees are diverse: multi-ethnic, multinational, multicultural, men and women, able-bodied and some with a disability and so forth. You should regard this as a positive strength, an asset to be used rather than a problem to be overcome.

Tangible and intangible benefits

Many benefits have been claimed from effective diversity management. The truth is that there are benefits, but not all the benefits claimed have yet been substantiated. Inevitably there will be a measure of judgement involved in deciding whether or not the diversity policies and procedures you incorporate into your everyday operation actually impact on the bottom line.

The benefits that organizations seek as they actively recruit and manage a diverse workforce may be summarized as follows:

- conformity to legal requirements
- wider search for talented people
- the management of labour costs
- operating in a diversely populated business environment
- good citizenship
- teamwork and a winning workforce.

The extent to which your organization can derive benefits from effective diversity management will depend on your circumstances. You must decide to what extent you are likely to benefit in each area, and this will guide your diversity strategy.

Legal requirements

Hitherto, the law has been primarily concerned with the elimination of discrimination against particular classes of people, for example women, ethnic minorities and disabled people. Such laws are particularly strong in the European Community, North America, Australia and New Zealand. In the USA there are also laws prohibiting discrimination on the grounds of age.

Organizations that operate on a worldwide basis find that when they run courses on managing diversity for managers it is necessary to include sections on the local legal situation. The efforts made by Schroders (in 33 countries) and by Reuters (in 98 countries) are particularly noteworthy. These companies do not focus solely on adherence to the law; the emphasis is on treating every individual with respect and providing opportunities for fair treatment for every employee. Such companies expect all their employees to treat all their business contacts with respect as well – and to be treated with respect by them. These companies certainly seek to abide by the law, but this is just a baseline from which they build effective 'people' policies.

For any company the legal requirements in each country or state will form a baseline for good practice, but if the resulting set of rules and procedures is not backed up by attention to people's attitudes within the organization – particularly at the higher levels – it will not be enough. It is outside the scope of this book to deal with legal requirements in detail. They are constantly changing and managers will need to keep abreast of developments in their own country or state.

> ▶ **The law is just a baseline from which to build effective people policies**

Reuters Limited operates with 17,000 employees in 217 cities and in 98 countries. The company has an active policy of respect for people, promoting both compliance with the law and good industrial relations. The legal situation in every country is closely monitored. During 1999-2000 a worldwide programme provided a short training course for every manager covering the management of diversity. The core content is provided centrally and this is supplemented by a presentation by a local employment lawyer in each country. Managers are also trained and briefed in the correct procedures to be followed in recruitment, selection and promotion. The company is particularly sensitive to the way its staff treat its customers. A contract can easily be lost by insensitive behaviour related to another person's gender, race or creed. This need for sensitivity applies as much to technicians servicing equipment as to people negotiating contracts or gathering news. As the company operates in so many countries, the staff must be able to deal effectively with local customers whose customs and practices may differ from the culture from which the staff member comes. The management development programme for an individual usually includes one or more foreign assignments.

Talented people

In evaluating the benefits one must compare, for example, the effect of recruiting from a diversity of people from the workforce against, say, employing only white Caucasian males. The evidence for opening up recruitment for women as well as men is overwhelming. Talent is not the exclusive preserve of white men. At one time companies used to recruit exclusively male engineers. The fact is that there are now many very capable and highly successful women engineers and scientists.

Talent does not lie exclusively with the white population – or the Asians, or the Chinese, or the Japanese. International companies seeking the best people learned long ago to look beyond the colour of skin, the nationality or cultural background of candidates for posts. On the other hand, it must be said that the standard of education varies from one country to another, and from one educational institution to another. International companies take these factors into account.

▶ **Talent is not the exclusive preserve of white males**

Lewisham Council, in London, serves a multi-ethnic population. The council has taken a number of steps to recruit from the whole range of its population, and to ensure that employees who are members of minority ethnic communities are given help in developing their abilities to the point where they can apply for, and obtain, more senior positions within the authority. Over the past few years this has enabled the council to recruit and manage a multi-ethnic workforce. A number of positive action initiatives have offered specific support for black and other minority ethnic staff in first-line management posts, and enabled them to progress into middle and senior management positions where they are currently (in April 2000) underrepresented.

Talent does not lie exclusively with the able-bodied, the young or the heterosexual members of the population although the employment policies of some organizations would seem to suggest this. Older workers may bring a maturity of approach and the benefit of experience to younger people – and to customers.

It must be said that in some cultures there are prejudices against some disabilities. Management will need to work harder to overcome these prejudices in these locations. Many organizations have recognized that their policies have been limiting their search for suitable people and they have made efforts to widen their search, often with tangible positive results. The obvious conclusion is that recruiting from a narrowly defined labour market, whether this is by default or by design, is unlikely to result in finding the best people.

Overall, many organizations have found that in recruitment, there have been tangible gains when the net is spread wider. The talent pool is greater. Some organizations have found, for example, that recruiting engineers from other European countries provides a source of well-qualified multilingual people.

Labour costs

Effective personnel management can potentially produce very real gains in terms of reduced labour turnover (lower recruitment and training costs) and reduced absenteeism. If your organization does not suffer unduly from these problems, there will clearly be little to gain in this area. On the other hand, it is possible for labour turnover to be too low because you have, in effect, created a cosy club of clones undisturbed by the external turbulence of racial and gender diversity.

Organizations with high levels of labour turnover and absenteeism need to investigate the underlying causes. Often these problems have been exacerbated by discrimination of one sort or another. This may take the form of harassment by the boss or by peers. People may feel they have been treated unfairly by the management, for example having been passed over for promotion or not given a fair share of privileges. You may be unaware of such practices in your organization, but if you have not investigated the reasons for absenteeism or high labour turnover, you could be living in a fools' paradise. You could also be exposing the organization to litigation on the grounds of discrimination or unfair dismissal. In many countries there are laws outlawing discrimination. In the UK, employees have brought successful discrimination cases where age has been a factor, but where gender has been the legal justification for the complaint.

> ▶ You may be unaware of discrimination in your organization, but ...

In large organizations it is worthwhile monitoring absenteeism and labour turnover by region, unit or section according to the way your firm is organized. Such monitoring may indicate areas where a deeper investigation would be beneficial.

The business environment

Organizations that deal directly with the public find that their staff and their documentation need to show respect for all kinds of people. This policy is hard to maintain if the company does not show respect for all its employees. Retailers and organizations that provide services to the public, such as the police and health authorities, are finding merit in seeking to recruit their employees from the whole population. The aim is to achieve, over time, ethnic and gender proportions in the workforce that mirror the population that these organizations serve.

Few organizations of any size now operate entirely in the domestic market. Often a substantial proportion of their customers is in other countries. Multinational companies are aware that when dealing with people in other countries, one must be aware of the local customs and practice, and of the expectations of people in business. First of all there are language problems. A literal translation on paper can fail to convey what the writer intended. It becomes even more critical when using an interpreter in business conversations. Quite often you will find that competent interpreters may not be familiar with the technical language you intend to employ in conversations. You must be particularly careful in the use of humour, especially satire. What may seem an obvious witticism to you may be taken literally by people from other cultures, with disastrous results in terms of misunderstanding.

Even when the language barrier is overcome, common business procedures and expectations may differ widely, particularly between, say, European and Oriental business people. The notion of respect for people that underlies this book is essential here. You need to respect your business associates in other countries and cultures. This means taking the trouble to understand their perspective, their customs and their expectations. There is, however, a potential pitfall here. You will be tempted to say, 'in general the Japanese (or the British, or the South Africans) are like this, therefore the person I am dealing with, who is Japanese (or British, or South African), will be like this'. It does not follow. Beware of generalizations and classifications. People differ from one another. Their behaviour and expectations depend on their background, but this is a complex picture and an individual may not behave as you would expect on a superficial knowledge of his or her background.

> **Few organizations of any size now operate entirely in the domestic market**

We all expect cultural differences when we are dealing with people in different continents, but there is ample research to show that cultural differences between people in the same continent are substantial. The emphasis throughout this book is that while taking note of race, creed, nationality, gender and disability, people must be treated with respect as individuals. The arguments set out in the previous paragraph apply equally to people within your organization who are from a particular group. A black person who was born and brought up in Glasgow, and whose mother and father were born and brought up in Scotland, is more likely to identify with Scotland than with his or her ethnic background.

If all the people in your organization are treated with respect and consideration, they are more likely to be inclined to treat your customers with respect as well. Quality management has become an important byword in many companies. This means providing goods and services that really meet the customers' needs. Many organizations have found that the way their staff treat their customers is just as important as the quality of the goods or services provided and the procedures employed. They have then learned that if you want your staff to treat your customers well, you must develop a culture in which people treat each other with respect and consideration.

> ▶ People need to be empowered to give good service to customers – and to each other

People need to be empowered to give good service to customers – and to each other. If your organization is dealing with a diversity of customers (at home or overseas), there are very real benefits to be gained by managing diversity effectively.

Good citizenship

For many companies, success depends as much on being a 'good corporate citizen' as on providing quality goods and services at reasonable costs. This applies particularly to those who have, as their customers, local or national governments of international bodies. Public bodies cannot be seen to do business with organizations that discriminate against people.

Public bodies themselves must also be seen to behave responsibly in respect of diversity issues. Elected bodies are forced to react to public opinion. Over the past century there have been increasing demands from women and ethnic minorities for equality of treatment, especially in the western world. This worldwide phenomenon has developed to the point where, in most countries, there are pressures from society as a whole to treat all people with fairness and respect irrespective of ethnic origin, creed or gender. As people's attitudes to age, gender, religion and disability vary from one society to another, what is regarded as fair treatment differs significantly from one country to another.

Organizations that interact directly with members of the public, for example the supply of gas, electricity, water and telephone services, and retailers must also take account of public opinion if they are to trade successfully. In the long run, the continued success of the organization may well depend, in part, on the effective management of diversity, not only within the ranks of employees but in relation to its dealings with its suppliers and customers.

Teamwork and a winning workforce

If you bring together a group of people with diverse backgrounds, you have the potential for a powerful team. The very diversity can be a source of strength. But it is a fallacy to believe that simply bringing them together will somehow weld them into an effective team. Without due care it is more likely that they will not function effectively. Over time, and with shared goals, they may form themselves into a team of some sort, but a group of people may or may not be a team. A team is a group of people who have learned to work in a particular way (*see* Chapter 10.)

> ▶ **There is merit in creating a teamwork culture**

If, in your organization, you have a number of relatively stable teams, there are steps you may take to help each of them to be effective. If, however, the teams in your organization tend to change quite often, there is merit in creating a teamwork culture, where each individual learns how to be an effective team member. We have pointed out elsewhere (Johnson and Redmond, 1997) that if you bring together a group of individuals trained in teamwork, and persuade them to 'buy in' to a common goal, you have a team that will function.

Our experience has shown that a teamwork culture can materially enhance the effectiveness of organizations. We share Dr Meredith Belbin's view (Belbin, 2000) that teams find it difficult to succeed in organizations where the overall culture is not supportive.

The European Agency for the Evaluation of Medicinal Products (EMEA) is a unique institution. About 200 people work together at Canary Wharf, managing an enormous variety of complex issues related to human and animal medicines. The Executive Director, Fernand Sauer (who is French), is responsible to the European Commission and the Council of Ministers and operates through a vast array of specialists and advisory committees. Fourteen nationalities work together on ▶

▶ a daily basis in relative harmony. The medical and veterinary fields are dominated by the English language so that much of the business is conducted in English, but there are very real cultural differences that people have to learn to respect if they are to work harmoniously together. Staff at the agency are employed on five-year renewable contracts, and as they are covered by the regulations of the European Commission, their employment is not regulated by UK law. There used to be age limits in recruitment advertisements, but these have gradually been raised without adverse comment.

The executive director and his senior colleagues have taken a number of steps to ensure that members of staff have a voice in the way the organization is run and the way people are treated. They instituted a 'culture group' to look at the aims and purposes of the agency and also a 'processes group' to look at where improvements were needed. These groups included staff as well as management. A number of constructive suggestions were made, including the introduction of a flexi-time scheme that has proved highly successful and has been accepted by all staff. One of the suggestions was concerned with how to make the agency more 'user-friendly' to visiting experts, providing them with somewhere to work and improving the arrangements for the payment of expenses. The culture is open, with managers welcoming suggestions and being prepared to act upon them. One member of staff said: 'Managing diversity is really about old-fashioned courtesy and being open with people.'

More information about the EMEA can be found on the web site at
http://www.eudra.org/emea.html

Pitfalls

The profitability of a company and its performance on the stock market is the result of complex interaction of factors. One of these factors is undoubtedly the effectiveness of the organization's workforce. However, because of the complex way in which these factors interact, it is often not possible to separate these effects. A programme to improve the motivation and effectiveness of the workforce takes time and money. All sorts of other factors may be at work – changes in the marketplace, raw material prices, transportation costs, fashion in buying habits, the activities of competitors and suppliers.

You may find that your programmes either do not work or have adverse effects. For example, if there is a high level of unemployment, resentment may build up among the majority indigenous population against minority groups. Unless they are handled with care, initiatives aimed at improving the equal treatment for minority groups could enhance this resentment. It is important to be seen to be scrupulously fair to every individual, whether employees or job applicants.

Particular care is also necessary if your organization decides to introduce positive discrimination of some kind. It is preferable to help people to acquire the knowledge and skills necessary to obtain employment and to make progress than to lower the standards for a particular group of people. Lowering the standards for employment or promotion means that the job may not be done so well, and it also means that those who are not given such opportunities can, rightly, feel aggrieved. Other people around the less able person will also be expected to 'carry' that individual – another potential source of resentment.

If you do introduce some positive action, help should be provided on the basis that the individual needs that help, not that the individual is a member of a disadvantaged group. Ideally, such help should be available to any employee, irrespective of race, gender and so forth. You may need to re-examine your criteria for recruitment (Chapter 4) and for promotion (Chapter 5) to eliminate items that are discriminatory against particular groups. This does not mean lowering the standards, but making them more appropriate to the job requirements. Furthermore, these standards will then apply equally to all applicants.

> **You may find that your programmes do not work, or have adverse effects**

When a need for training and development is identified for individuals in minority or disadvantaged groups, look around to see if others have similar needs before offering such opportunities only to people in the 'disadvantaged' group. For example, at one time it was popular to point out that many women lacked 'assertiveness'. A number of assertiveness training courses were set up exclusively for women. Later it was realised that (a) not all women lacked assertiveness, and (b) there were men who needed assertiveness training. If you believe that members of a disadvantaged group lack language skills, consider whether people who are not members of this group also need help with language skills.

The key imperative is to consider the needs of each individual, and not simply to deal with the needs of particular groups of people. The culture change to an empowered organization where every person counts is a tough one, but the rewards are there in terms of productivity, waste reduction, continuous improvement and quality.

A manufacturing company in the UK was in the process of completely re-equipping a particular plant. The old plant had been in place for 20 years and although it still worked, it was inefficient and labour costs were high. At the heart of the new plant were gleaming stainless steel vessels and a computer system with double back-up provision. The new plant needed only just over 100 people to operate, whereas the old plant needed 300. But those selected to work on the new plant had to be effective team workers. The company organized a series of teamwork workshops by shift. One group of workers was on permanent nights. Included in this group were a number of Asian workers and a Sikh. Most members of the group were reticent and slow to take part in the workshop, but eventually their confidence grew and they all took part. The white members of the group needed encouragement as well as the Asians and the Sikh gentleman. The workshop was a success and the company went on to reap the rewards of its investment in plant and people.

Progress checklist

[?] Have you considered the likely benefits of effective diversity management policies and practices?

[?] Do you have mechanisms in place to ensure that in every country where you operate you are aware of the legal requirements in relation to diversity?

[?] Have you ensured that all your employees, especially managers, are fully aware of the laws' demands and trained to operate within these parameters?

[?] Have you considered the way that diversity management can help to contain your employment costs?

[?] Have you considered carefully the business environment and the extent to which diversity management can improve your effectiveness in dealing with customers and suppliers?

[?] Does 'good citizenship' have any impact on your business? Are you taking steps to ensure that your organization's behaviour is seen to be above reproach, for example in the matter of diversity management?

[?] Have you taken steps to ensure that your multicultural teams are fully effective?

? Are you aware of the pitfalls and the steps you will need to take to avoid them?

? Do you want the people in your organization to be a 'winning' workforce?

3

Priorities for action

Comprehensive or selective policies

Effective diversity management involves attention to policies and procedures in a number of key areas related to the way people are treated within your organization:

- recruitment
- terms and conditions of service
- selection
- induction and initial training
- communication channels
- performance appraisal
- personal development
- reorganizations and redeployment
- redundancies.

If diversity management is to extend to the way your people interact with business contacts, especially customers, this philosophy must be included in all the above areas. If you have a quality management programme, treating people with respect should be a key factor.

In some organizations, particularly those where you need to gain widespread support for policy changes (for example within trade unions, professional bodies, charitable bodies), you may decide to adopt an incremental approach. Such organizations generally respond to internal pressure groups and this may be a way forward, rather than seeking to impose change from the top. This procedure does not mean that leadership from the top is unnecessary, it is about how that leadership is exercised.

A lobby group may be formed, for example, initially to link people for mutual support (for example a women's group, or a group for lesbians and gays, or for black people in the organization). As the group gains strength you may find that it is a useful source of information and advice about how the people in that group are treated.

▶ **Consider the way your people interact with business contacts**

You may want to grant them the ability to meet in one of your rooms, and to advertise their activities on the intranet or in the company newsletter.

In a large organization, representatives could be elected to serve on a forum so that you could consult the group members on a more formal basis. If the group behaves responsibly, you may want to elevate the status of the forum to an advisory committee. Such an advisory committee would have no power as such, but it could make recommendations to the management on how matters could be improved for group members. If you adopt this approach you must decide the extent to which you want to encourage such activities and the way they will link into your existing structures and procedures, such as negotiations with trade unions or links with works councils.

You will need to decide whether you wish to embrace diversity policies comprehensively, or whether you will be content to deal with the legal requirements plus any area that seems to present particular problems or opportunities. Such a decision will influence your policies and procedures in each case. In the remainder of this book it is assumed that the management is keen on a comprehensive approach, but it will be easy to adapt the advice to specific priorities if required.

A plan of action to implement either approach should be based on an analysis of the current situation. You will need to collect some data. It is not enough to rely on your own impressions plus those of senior colleagues.

Look at the existing information first. You will need to get an up-to-date picture by asking people questions.

What information?

The starting point is to collect information about your workforce, in terms of profiles of gender, race, age and disability. You will find that such information is even more useful if it can be broken down further, for example by grade, operational unit and function. For instance, in many organizations, women in the human resource function find it easier to get promotion than those in production. If you look at operational units, it may be relevant to compare the ratio of people from ethnic minorities in the workforce with that in the local labour force.

You will also find it useful to monitor figures on recruitment, promotion and labour turnover. Do you have very few applicants from women, or black people, or Chinese, although these form a large proportion of the pool of labour for these jobs? Does it appear difficult for women to get top jobs? Are few Asian people promoted to middle management in relation to their numbers at lower levels? Do you find that the labour turnover is highest for a particular group of people? You cannot rely on hearsay; you need reliable numbers.

▶ Collect data about diversity in your organization

Another factor to consider is language. Do you know how many 'first' languages your people speak? By 'first' language in this context we mean the language that the individual uses most naturally. It is the one most likely to be used in speaking to family and friends of the same race. A recent immigrant may still speak his original language as a first language, and the indigenous one as a second language. But a second or third generation immigrant will probably use the indigenous language as the first language. The extent to which people can speak English in an English-speaking country, for example, may be important for safety reasons. It has been said that in a panic situation, people think in their own language. One way or another, you need to get a grip on the extent to which you have a language problem in your organization.

Your marketing department will have data on the customers your organization serves and you may wish to take this into account. For example, if your organization serves a community with a particular ethnic mix, you may wish to consider this in your recruitment policies. Companies that operate overseas have found that it is usually essential to have, as part of the workforce, competent local people recruited from the indigenous population to interface with customers, whether individual or corporate clients.

Quite apart from numerical data you will need information about people's behaviour in the organization and about their perceptions. Often what people perceive will indicate where investigation of behaviour is required. If people say they believe that some harassment is taking place, for example, this is a matter you will need to investigate. Ask employees what they think about the organization, the management and the culture. Collect information about the extent to which people experience particular types of harassment, for example on the basis of race, gender, sexuality, age or disability. Include opinions about the way your employees interact with people in other organizations or members of the public. You may find it helpful to seek the views of people outside the organization, people who deal with your firm.

▶ **You need information about people's behaviour and their perceptions**

Existing information

Analyzing and collating data that is already available, for example from employee records, may enable you to produce profiles of gender, race, disability and age, but the reliability of this data must be subject to scrutiny. Often information collected for one purpose proves unsatisfactory when used for another. Gender and age data will probably be useful. However, it is not unknown for people to lie about their age for one reason or another. Hopefully, this kind of error will not be statistically significant.

In collecting data about people with disabilities, however, there are very real problems. In many cases, successful people with a disability have no desire to have this disability recorded. It is often of no help to them to have this on record. The likelihood is that the formal figures will underestimate the number of disabled people in the workforce. You may need to conduct a new survey (see below).

Bear in mind that a disability may not be obvious. We can usually spot someone who has difficulty in walking, seeing or hearing. But sometimes disabilities are not easy to discern. Some people with walking, hearing or seeing difficulties often cope so well that their disability is not noticed. Never assume that any individual is without a disability.

If your organization has been collecting racial data, you may be able to use this. The problem here is who decides how to record a person's race? On the whole it is probably better to ask each individual to which race he or she belongs. As mentioned earlier, it is important to distinguish between race and nationality. Some organizations have found it useful simply to distinguish between black and white people. Another key question is why you wish to know. If you observe, or if it is reported to you, that a certain group – based on colour, race, creed or nationality – appears to be treated unfairly by your organization, it is probably wise to collect information that illuminates the problem area.

There are a number of sources of information about the external situation, for example from labour force surveys, population surveys, consumer surveys and employers' organizations. Many large retailers now collect information about their customers through loyalty card systems. We understand that in the London Borough of Lewisham, gender and race have been monitored for many years. We came across one organization where human resource managers in one department refused to provide any numerical information at all to head office about people with disabilities on the grounds that this breached confidentiality – even though the head office had not asked for individuals to be named or identified in any way. It must be stressed that without measurement there can be no effective management.

Collecting new information

If you want to collect people's opinions about the current situation you may conduct a survey (see below) or hold a series of discussion meetings with groups of people. If you have a very large organization it may be possible to collect some impressions by holding meetings with representative groups, say within each division or in each country. Properly organized, it is possible to hold larger meetings, with groups being formed within these. A full discussion of such meetings is outside the scope of this book (*see* Chapter 9, Johnson and Redmond, 1998).

Such gatherings may be useful in pointing up potential issues and indicating some of the methods that may be used to improve the situation, although they do not generally provide reliable quantitative data for which a survey is required.

You may ask questions in a number of ways. You may conduct face-to-face interviews, distribute paper and pencil questionnaires or invite people to answer questions on-line on your company intranet. The latter method is being used successfully by an increasing number of organizations. The use of the intranet is of particular value when the workforce is widely distributed. International organizations find the method especially valuable. The use of the intranet assumes that all employees can gain access to a terminal and that each person has a personal password to enter the system.

> **In using questionnaires, the degree of confidentiality must be made clear**

Before completing any questionnaire, whether on-line or on paper, the individual must be convinced that the results will not be abused in any way. This means that the degree of confidentiality must be clear, along with the purpose of the questions, and how the answers will be used. Some organizations have begun by having discussions with the workforce about the survey long before it takes place. By involving people in discussions at an early stage, the purpose of the investigation can be made clear, and the content of the survey will often be refined as employees make useful suggestions for improvement.

The director of an international organization was keen to improve the morale of staff and the way people related to one another and with business contacts. He and his senior colleagues were keen to involve all the staff in a change programme. They appointed a number of work groups to tackle different aspects of the organization's task, how it should be carried out, how people should work together and how human resource policies should be implemented. Among the many improvements, the staff developed a survey to be used on the intranet. Almost everyone in the organization completed the survey questionnaire. The data enabled the organization to monitor the effectiveness of its human resource policies and the level of teamwork in the organization.

Employees involved in the design of a survey are more likely to take it seriously and to answer questions conscientiously. The value of survey results is totally dependent on the quality of the answers. To maintain trust, the results of the survey – however painful – must be made available to the people who completed the questionnaires.

The motivation of the person completing the questionnaire is important. As mentioned above, many people with disabilities do not want this noted. To obtain reliable figures, you will need to create a culture in which a person with a disability suffers no discrimination, and is regarded as a valuable member of the community. Then you will need to convince everyone that collecting this information has no ulterior motive but to improve your performance in dealing with disability. Only when these conditions are satisfied will such a survey give reliable results.

A survey of your workforce must not be undertaken lightly. The way must be prepared, the purpose clearly explained, the questions carefully chosen and tested, and people convinced that the exercise will be beneficial to the workforce, not just to the organization.

It must never be forgotten that a survey is a method of intervention. By that we mean that when you conduct a survey, you raise the expectation that something will result from it – more than just the answers. It is inferred that there is a problem to be addressed and that management is collecting information as a basis for dealing with it. If you collect the data, publish the results and then do nothing about the problem, you have most probably made matters worse. The advice is, if you are not prepared to take action on the problems that are revealed, for goodness sake don't conduct a survey.

Deciding priorities

Your decisions about priorities will probably be based on three main considerations:

● the information you have,

● the problems you perceive

● your business imperatives.

The information you collect should give you clear indications of the extent to which:

● staff from all cultural backgrounds, age, gender and disability are integrated into the organization and represented at various levels of responsibility;

● people consider that the organization is fair in its treatment of every individual, especially in respect of recruitment, selection, development, deployment and promotion procedures;

- discrimination and harassment have been eliminated;
- your organization is safe from any legal action on the grounds of unfair discrimination;
- the organization is well regarded by customers, the community and other business contacts in its dealings with people.

This information will enable you to determine whether or not you need to take any corrective action. For example, you may wish to promote the development of underrepresented minority groups in the workforce, encourage more women to seek development and promotion, tackle institutional racism or provide opportunities for older workers.

The 1980s was a busy decade for B&Q, a major DIY retailer in the UK, with stores opening across the country. During the 1990s the store numbers remained static at about 280, but sales space was increased dramatically through the opening of B&Q Warehouses that were typically three times the size of the average B&Q store.

B&Q is committed to the value of 'respect for people'. Successfully managed diversity in B&Q creates a balance of skill, style and ideas that reflects the customer base. The more diverse the range of perspectives, the more innovative the problem solving. Each B&Q store aims to reflect its local community, and by being a good neighbour, the store can capture local knowledge and culture. Diversity management, in addition to being both morally right and socially desirable, has an overwhelming business case. B&Q no longer uses the term 'equal opportunities' to describe its approach, preferring the term 'diversity'. In taking an 'inclusive' approach in terms of 'respect for people', the emphasis is on the individual and not an exclusive list of groups of disadvantaged people. Customers are the key to the company's diversity strategy. B&Q is internally driven to exceed its business expectations, and the diversity strategy must be measurable in business terms.

In the late 1980s, B&Q recognized that its workforce was predominantly young and that staff turnover was highest among the younger staff. In 1989, it opened a store in Macclesfield, and another in Exmouth in 1990, staffed entirely by people over 50 years of age. It was anticipated that older people were more likely to be home-owners and to have done DIY themselves. They would probably have an interest in and some knowledge of DIY. Both stores were highly successful, and the company began to encourage applications from older workers, often formerly trades people, in all its stores. The company now believes that stores which have a workforce with a mix of ▶

▶ age, experience and background can and do offer the quality of service excellence that customers have come to expect. Martin Toogood, Managing Director, has stated: 'For ten years, the business has benefited from the age-diverse workforce resulting from its policy of employing older workers as well as younger ones. Independent studies show customers recognize and value the customer service we offer as a result. 'For us, it's been a win-win situation.'

B&Q is now trying to ensure that management teams become more age diverse, recognizing the benefits this could bring to the organization. Since 1998, the company has removed the top age of 25 for graduate recruits to the retail operation. This will enable B&Q to select from a wider pool of applicants. Beyond the normal retirement age of 60, both new and existing employees can be given opportunities to continue on fixed-term contracts.

B&Q considers that the benefits of its diversity policies are a larger pool of talent from which to recruit, a mixed-age workforce that reflects its customer base, increased customer satisfaction, reduced staff turnover, resulting in reduced recruitment costs, and a wide range of experience and expertise among its employees.

If any of these problems is seen to impact on your organizational performance this will probably be your top priority. This assumes that you are satisfied that you have made every effort to comply with any laws on discrimination or harassment that apply. If you have not done this, it must be an overriding priority. Your procedures must be reviewed as a matter of urgency, and your managers trained to implement them without fail. If attention to particular areas can enhance your organizational performance, this can become a second priority area. If the image of your organization is important, either in the eyes of your customers or backers, this is another compelling reason for action.

Once you have determined priority areas for action there is merit in devising an overall strategy. If your organization's culture needs a substantial change, linking the change process with definite business objectives will help to keep the process on track. A learning-needs analysis may be required, perhaps covering all existing staff, but especially managers, recruiters and trainers.

Action plan

The typical action plan will include the elements listed below. The relative importance of each component of your plan will depend upon your priorities and the nature of the organizational culture change you wish to bring about. You may, of course, decide to focus on specific issues (for example race, age or gender) at the outset, rather than starting with a comprehensive approach, but the basic steps will be the same.

1. Secure top management commitment.
2. Collect information.
3. Recruitment and selection.
4. Terms and conditions.
5. Induction and initial training.
6. Communication channels.
7. Performance appraisal.
8. Training and development.
9. Reorganization and redeployment.
10. Maintain momentum.

The start of any worthwhile change programme involves securing top management commitment – this may take several hours, or even days, of discussion. You may need to take the most senior group of executives away on a weekend workshop, perhaps with a facilitator. If any member of the top team is not behind the approach you propose to take, this will cause problems. In the first instance you may simply agree to explore the issues and conduct a survey. Remember, however, that conducting any survey will arouse expectations and you will need to be prepared to respond.

The information that you collect must include people's perceptions. The results will need to be considered by the top management team and should influence further action. You must be prepared to make the results of any survey public.

A comprehensive diversity policy is founded on the notion of respect for every individual. Review policies and practices to ensure that they are in line with your new aims and objectives. For example, you may need to ensure that when you seek to fill posts your advertising will reach people in ethnic minorities, or older workers, or people with disabilities, and be attractive to them. Ensure that your employment terms do not discriminate against single-sex couples, for example in respect of pensions or leave entitlement. Include specific reference to the avoidance of harassment or indirect discrimination in initial training. You may want to include mentoring as one of the tools to help members of a disadvantaged group to develop their potential. Details of these policies are discussed in later chapters. Ensure that policies on redeployment and redundancies do not discriminate unfairly against older workers.

Review your channels of communication. We know that if you do not take special steps to make it easy for people to report acts of discrimination, bullying or harassment, you will not find out about them until the incident has caused someone to resign or to appeal to an external body for compensation or redress. To bring about a major culture change you may need to initiate a set of respecting diversity workshops, starting from the top and cascading down. At the very least you will probably need to ensure that every manager is aware of the new policy and trained to put it into practice in the everyday work of the organization.

> ▶ A comprehensive diversity policy is founded on respect for every individual

Some companies have found it helpful to appoint and train some members of staff as 'mediators' (*see* Chapter 6). All of your employees will need training and development and it is important to ensure that there is no direct discrimination in the training on offer, and no indirect discrimination through the way the training is provided.

Periods when the company needs to reorganize the way duties are allocated are always stressful for staff. Many organizations are particularly bad at handling the communications in these circumstances. There may be a positive outcome in that these changes may provide opportunities for redistributing responsibilities in ways that make full use of the talents of every member of staff. You must be careful to avoid discrimination, especially when redundancies are involved.

Finally, how do you keep the thing going? The top management team will need to appoint someone to monitor progress and report back at intervals. You will want to monitor what is going on through periodic surveys, and it is wise to organize exit interviews, as these can be a means of alerting management to issues that employees may be reluctant to raise in other circumstances. You may get some ideas on monitoring from benchmarking, that is comparing your organization's performance with the best in your industrial sector. If you find it difficult to get sufficient information to undertake such comparisons, identify criteria against which your organization can be measured. You should include hard and soft criteria. Hard criteria are concerned with numbers, for example the ratio of women in various positions, the ratio of black people promoted to managerial positions, the ratio of Asians relative to the local population, the number of tribunal cases for harassment. Alongside this go the soft measures – people's perceptions about fairness, equality of opportunity and the like.

The most senior executives will need to set an example at all times and be prepared to get involved in programmes to convince people that the organization is serious about accepting and respecting every employee and every person who comes into contact with the organization. You may find it helpful to have these activities overseen by a steering group led by a board member, with representatives from line management, human resources and employee representatives. This will help you to manage the change effectively and to gain wide support for the new policies and procedures. A person can be appointed as a diversity manager to co-ordinate these activities and to promote improved diversity management.

> ▶ **Identify criteria against which your organization can be measured. You should include hard and soft criteria**

Progress checklist

- ? Are you and your senior colleagues prepared to consider carefully the current situation in your organization with respect to diversity?

- ? If necessary, are you prepared to put some time and effort into improving the situation?

- ? Have you considered the information you will need to make sound business decisions, and how you will get it?

- ? Have you collected the information you require?

- ? Have you considered your current position and your business needs, and on this basis identified priorities for action?

- ? Does the incremental approach have relevance for your organization?

- ? Do you have a credible action plan?

4

Recruitment

Finding the best people

Recruitment is the process by which you seek to engage the staff that your organization requires to function effectively. In forming the contract of employment there are effectively two parties – the employer and the employee. There is a choice to be made by both parties. In areas of high unemployment the employer may consider that the prospective employee has little choice, but in areas of full employment it may be the prospective employees who have the choice. In some geographical areas organizations have difficulty in recruiting suitable employees because of the competition for labour when the economy is buoyant.

Over recent years there have been increasing pressures, including legal constraints, to prevent employers selecting employees on the basis of criteria that are unrelated to the requirements of the job. The employer that seeks to manage diversity in a comprehensive manner will need to ensure that in recruitment there is no discrimination on the grounds of gender, marital status, sexual orientation, colour, race, nationality, ethnic or national origin, age or any irrelevant factor. This assumes that the individual has a valid right to be employed in the work location. Exceptions can be made where there is a genuine job requirement for authenticity or with regard to public taste and decency.

But the aim is more than simply avoiding discrimination. It is about making sure that you have trawled through the appropriate labour market and found the best people you can get to fill your jobs. There are at least three different types of labour market. For a factory or retail store in a small town where specialist skills are not required for the most part, most of the posts may be filled by people from the local population. However, in some sectors there are specific skill requirements and the labour market for those skills may be the people who work (or who have recently worked) within that particular sector. Examples are in oil exploration, finance, and construction. Thirdly, there are skills that are not specific to industries but to professions. Examples include accountancy, marketing and human resource management. Naturally this classification is not watertight, but it is a useful way to look at many recruitment situations.

> **The aim is more than simply avoiding discrimination**

BAE Systems (formed by the merger of British Aerospace and part of the General Electric Company in 1999) is a major defence systems company with more than 100,000 employees in the UK, the USA, Scandinavia, Italy, France, Germany and Australia. The current policy is to operate through joint ventures with companies outside the UK rather than setting up new BAE operations.

Over recent years there has been a major shift in culture within British Aerospace, led by the former Chief Executive, now Chairman, Sir Richard Evans. The company is taking a global view of its workforce, responding to social change and creating a vision of tomorrow's employer, where innovation and developing people's full potential are the order of the day.

The British Aerospace change programme was based on five core values: performance as the key to winning; partnership with its business contacts to secure the future; customers as the highest priority; innovation and technology to provide the competitive edge; and people – 'our greatest strength'. Creating the new people strategy involved considerable discussions during 1998–1999 and recognized a number of key challenges, for example the need to develop a culture ▶

▶ of trust and commitment while maintaining a lean and cost-conscious operation. The strategy also involved commitment to more family-friendly policies and to the development of a learning organization, recognizing that 'there's more to work than turning up on time'.

Historically, the company has attracted predominantly white males into the business, but the organization is making real efforts to overcome this imbalance. In recruiting graduates, for example, it has succeeded in attracting a higher percentage of female engineering graduates than the percentage of graduate engineers that are female. The company supports initiatives to bring more women into science and engineering. Women are now finding their way into senior positions in the company.

BAE recruits many graduates from Europe, for example from Holland, Spain, Ireland, Portugal, Italy, Germany and France.

Broadly speaking, the recruitment process can be divided into the following stages:

- decision to seek new staff
- advertising for applicants, generating enquiries
- provision of information/application forms to enquirers
- selection of applicants for further consideration
- shortlist selection, often based on preliminary interviews
- final selection, often by interview.

Your selection process may not follow this precise pattern, but the advice provided in the following section will help you to avoid serious pitfalls.

Need for recruitment

Before embarking on a recruitment process, use the following checklist.

- review the organization, and its need for people. Do not do this behind closed doors unless there is a very clear need for secrecy on commercial grounds. Involve your staff, particularly those most closely affected;
- allocate tasks and responsibilities, firstly among the people you have, so that you can assess the workload and where more help is required;

- identify skill gaps in your organization, looking to the future as well as to the current situation;

- draw up job profiles that will both get the job done and bring in the necessary skills;

- identify the kind of people who can fill your job vacancies, ensuring that you have not unintentionally included requirements that are not really necessary and may discriminate against particular individuals or groups;

- recruit against the specifications you have drawn up.

Descriptions of these processes can be found in human resource management textbooks. Older textbooks, however, may not cover the discrimination issues in sufficient detail. If one of the key tasks of your organization is to interface with a multi-ethnic public, or with other organizations that employ people with cultural diversity, then this ability to interface becomes a key skill. If your retail customers include a large number of older people, it might make sense to ensure that the composition of your sales staff reflects this aspect of diversity.

> **Before compiling job profiles, consider existing staff**

This will enable you to draw up profiles of the kinds of people who can fill the jobs identified. In drawing up these profiles make sure that they are not culture or knowledge biased. This is particularly important when you draw up the information for enquirers and application forms, design any tests or set up interviews for selection (see below).

Beware of drawing up a person specification that includes requirements that are not, in fact, essential. In the past it has been customary to put age limits on certain types of posts. This is rarely justifiable. You may have drawn up a specification that excludes people with particular types of disability. In one organization, senior people convinced themselves that as some severely disabled people might need a lot of help in the workplace, to employ a disabled person effectively doubled the labour costs. They therefore felt there was little they could do about the problem. In fact, most disabled people who attend the workplace need little help from other people provided sensible and reasonable adjustments are made to the workplace and equipment.

Are you recruiting someone to simply fill a particular job vacancy? The likelihood is that within six months to a year that job will be different! The traditional approach of a job vacancy based on a job description and person specification is still valid, but it needs to be treated with some caution in the rapidly changing world of work. It is often better to think in terms of recruiting and promoting people into a cadre of employees performing a range of tasks, or better still a group of people performing a range of roles and exercising a range of responsibilities.

The tendency is to specify much higher levels of skill, knowledge and understanding than are actually required to do the job effectively. This has the effect of eliminating people who may have the ability to do the job, but who do not pass your selection procedures. Be careful about specifying local educational or vocational qualifications. You may find well-qualified immigrants in the labour force, but whose qualifications were not obtained in your country. It is not always easy to estimate the worth of qualifications if you are not familiar with them (this may well be true of qualifications awarded in your own country). Some organizations find that many graduate engineers from Europe are highly versatile and well educated, and that many software specialists in India are of a high calibre. This may influence where you advertise, but every individual must be assessed on his or her ability.

▶ **Most disabled people who attend the workplace need little help from other people**

Because the syllabus may vary markedly from one higher educational institution to another, you may find, at interview, that graduates from a particular institution bring a wealth of relevant knowledge to your organization. Again, assess each applicant individually and carefully. Tests of ability and psychological tests are covered in Chapter 5, but here it is important to recognize that they cannot be a substitute for a balanced recruitment process. However, they can form an effective part of the process provided they are well chosen, properly executed and interpreted.

Once you have decided on the jobs you want to fill and the person profiles required, be careful to see that the recruitment process reflects this at each stage, without introducing direct or indirect discrimination against anybody who might legitimately apply.

Advertising

Advertising for applicants can take many forms. Advertisement in newspapers, magazines, posters, radio and television has been used for many years. Private and public recruitment services are also used extensively to stimulate applications. In some industries word of mouth and family connections have been used extensively to generate enquiries. The latter methods are wide open to abuse and should never be used exclusively. The tendency will be for the jobs to be filled with people like the ones you already employ, to the exclusion of people who do not belong to those groups.

Nowadays the internet is proving a fertile source of job applications. Jobs advertised on the internet may be applied for by telephone, letter or, most often, e-mail. The same level of care is needed in framing advertisements, constructing application forms and dealing with applications. These jobs are usually advertised on a worldwide basis and you may expect a response from almost any part of the world. At the time of writing the internet use is expanding at an enormous rate, and many jobs will be filled by this means. The use of the internet through television sets and mobile phones using Wireless Access Protocol will enhance this growth. You will expect the more computer-literate people to apply this way.

> **Recruiting by word of mouth is open to abuse**

The employer must avoid direct discrimination, for example by including a gender or race requirement in a job advertisement. If a local qualification is mentioned, it should be made clear that equivalent qualifications will be acceptable.

If you suspect that your advertisements are reaching only a section of the potential labour force, you will need to monitor the number of applicants in relation to the composition of the labour force that forms your potential pool of labour. For example, if you are recruiting from a particular district where there is a significant number of people from an ethnic minority group, you may wish to look at the ratio of applicants from that minority group. If you find that the ratio is much lower than you would expect, you will need to investigate why this is so. There may be a number of reasons for this, including:

● your advertisements may not reach people in the group concerned (for example in an ethnic minority);

● your company may have a poor image as an employer of people in that group;

● the response you require is more difficult for people from the minority group;

● the advertisement appears to make unrealistic demands.

Migrants who have not yet acquired fluency in the local language may not read the newspapers you advertise in or the radio programme you use for recruitment. This is likely to be a problem mainly for lower level-jobs. Some organizations have tried to overcome this by making vacancies known through community organizations or publications that serve ethnic minorities. This is, however, likely to be at best a temporary solution. Experience has shown that once people have learned to speak the local language, it is often better to use local newspapers read by everyone for the lower-level jobs.

After a time immigrants tend to identify more with the local community and to take an interest in local matters. Community groups can often be a source of help and advice in determining the problems of recruitment and how to overcome them.

If your organization has a poor image in the eyes of a particular group, this may deter applications. The first thing to investigate is the extent to which this perception accords with reality. Many organizations that have traditionally been dominated by men (for example heavy engineering, construction, finance, law enforcement) have a culture hostile to women. No amount of clever advertising will overcome this. The organization must tackle the internal culture first, bring in some capable women, and gradually transform itself.

> ▶ A poor image in the eyes of a particular group may deter applications

The same is true of the other groups that suffer discrimination. Racism in the law enforcement agencies is a real problem in many countries around the world. Discrimination on grounds of sexuality is another widespread problem.

If, however, the organization has made real strides in overcoming discrimination and harassment of specific groups, steps must be taken to demonstrate this to the public and to potential employees. For example, organizations that seek to recruit women graduates or graduates from minority groups often produce literature that highlights successful people in their organization who come from these groups. Some organizations consider it helpful to declare that they are 'equal opportunity employers' both in their advertisements and in their literature.

In November 1999 the UK mail service issued a flyer headed 'Need extra cash at Christmas?' inviting people to 'Come and join the Royal Mail during the Christmas rush'. Significantly, there was a prominent footnote stating: 'Royal Mail is an Equal Opportunities Employer and welcomes applications from all section of the community. Suitably qualified applicants with disability will be shortlisted for interview.'

Organizations that wish to encourage applications from local people who are disabled or who belong to ethnic minorities may seek 'role models' from within the organization. The success of these role models can be publicized in a variety of ways. One must be careful, however, as role models seem to fall into two types – some people seem to thrive on the publicity, occasionally to excess, while others do not feel comfortable with the limelight and do not want their activities to be paraded in public.

> ▶ People will not respond if the advertisement stipulates unrealistic or irrelevant requirements

The purpose of any advertisement is to generate awareness, create interest, engender a desire and promote an action – usually an enquiry by letter, a telephone call or a personal visit. The way that your organization responds at this first encounter is crucial (see below for some ideas on this response). As indicated previously, people will not respond if the advertisement stipulates unrealistic or irrelevant requirements that they are unable to meet.

Response to enquiries

Examine your organization's response to the initial enquiry. Are the telephonists and receptionists trained to respond in an encouraging manner – and not to gasp at a foreign-looking or sounding person? Is the literature you send out simple, readable and acceptable to all the kinds of people who might respond? Are your application forms suitable for everybody? Or do they ask a Muslim for his 'Christian' name? All this needs to be vetted for freedom from bias.

If you are seeking to recruit from recent immigrants you may wish to include documentation in their own language, particularly if fluency in the local language is not a requirement for the job. Obviously the person must be able to communicate at a minimal level, even in humble jobs.

For many people, completing an application form is a daunting prospect. This is particularly acute if the form is not user-friendly. You need to ensure that the form is designed for applicants who may not share your first language, and for whom some of the terms are unclear. You could arrange to trial the form with the kinds of people you wish to attract. For example, if you have some Asian employees and want to employ more, ask some of your employees to help you to make your paperwork more user-friendly to that group. If there is one particular language that is spoken by the racial minority in your area, you might consider translating some parts of the form and the descriptive literature that accompanies it.

> **For many people, completing an application form is a daunting prospect**

The first sift

If you receive a large number of applications for very few jobs your first task is to select a list of potentially suitable candidates for the final stage of selection. Do not eliminate people on trivial grounds based on what is written on their application form or said on the telephone. Beware of bias due to the person's gender, accent or postal or zip code. Do not reject someone because the spelling of the name suggests a 'foreigner'.

Study of a completed application form can provide only clues and some preliminary evidence about the applicant's career pattern and attainments, powers of self-expression and range of interests. You may be able to find indications of how the individual has been able to use the opportunities presented in his education and work experience. The problem with most written application forms is that they require the individual to read the instructions and, often, to compose sentences. This is fine if you require these skills in the job, but if not, you could be dismissing, at an early stage, somebody capable of good work, but with limited literacy skills in your language.

A form that consists mainly of tick boxes may help the person with limited literacy skills, but it will limit the extent to which you will be able to judge his interests and ability for self-expression. Nowadays many more people are applying for posts through the internet. If you seek applications through this route you must be careful in drawing up (a) the job and person specification, and (b) the questionnaire that you invite people to complete on-line.

Some personnel officers study the completed application form line by line, looking for gaps in the narrative that might indicate periods of illness – or imprisonment! It is always difficult to interpret what an individual says about the jobs she has held and her responsibilities. You can expect any candidate worth her salt to make the best of whatever experiences she has had. But in some cultures an individual may well feel that it is not her place to extol her own virtues. If you are forced to select a limited number of people to invite for interview or selection tests, avoid giving the appearance of bias or discrimination. Be prepared to justify your selection on the basis of sensible criteria.

Shortlist selection

Once a reasonable number of people has been selected for further consideration they may be asked to sit tests and/or attend for interview. Written tests are a particular minefield. It is very easy for bias to be introduced, and there is ample evidence to show that gender and cultural bias can be a problem.

Many tests are developed in a particular culture and when used outside that culture they may give unreliable results. Many of the motivational theories that underlie some tests have been developed in the USA, and there is ample evidence from cultural studies that the norms for the USA do not correspond to those in other cultures. We have even come across selection tests that require 'general knowledge'. The problem is that what may be general knowledge to some people is a closed book to others.

> ▶ Tests developed in a particular culture may give unreliable results when used outside that culture

We came across one organization, a public body, where a 'general knowledge' questionnaire was used early in the selection process in recruitment. There were several questions about male-dominated sports and interests. Women applicants regularly scored lower marks than male applicants until the anomaly was noticed and the questions revised to remove this male bias.

Some tests implicitly rely on knowledge, for example of the nuances of language, culture or national characteristics. People from particular groups (women, ethic minorities) may not share this knowledge, for example if men from a particular cultural background have devised the tests.

If you decide to use any personality or intelligence tests you will need to be sure that (a) the results are valid for the cultures of the applicants, and (b) the results are relevant to the job and to the person profiles against which the selection is being made.

A similar problem can arise in the preliminary interview situation. The interviewers, in all good faith, may be framing questions in anticipation of answers consistent with their own cultural background. If the interviewee does not share this cultural background, he may not fare well. Experience has shown that open questions are more effective in this situation, enabling the individual to display knowledge of the subject and the ability to think, without the constraints of a pre-conceived answer. But even open questions may be framed in such a way that a particular type of reply is sought. It is preferable to include questions that enable people to talk about relevant experiences from which the interviewer can recognize that appropriate

> **Recruiting inappropriate people can increase labour turnover**

skills and understanding have been deployed. Such questions are particularly helpful to people who have not shared the interviewer's experiences in society and employment.

The law in many countries prohibits the interviewer from asking questions that are discriminatory (for example about marital status and the care of children) and you will need to ensure that the managers and human resource staff who recruit people are familiar with these limitations.

Final selection

If the final selection depends on an interview, the comments above still apply. In the final analysis, in many countries you can be called to account for your actions if an individual claims that you showed discrimination during the recruitment process. All you can do is to ensure that you have complied with the law and that you have documented your reasons for decisions at each stage.

The most important question you have to answer is, do you have the best people for the jobs – and do you manage to retain them for a reasonable period? There are many reasons why people leave organizations and if you have a serious labour turnover problem this will need investigation. One reason could be because you are not recruiting the right people.

Progress checklist

- [?] Have you developed an approach to recruitment that ensures you get the best people?

- [?] Does this approach avoid discrimination against particular groups of people?

- [?] Do your procedures ensure that you consider the organization and the people you need before you rush out to recruit?

- [?] Are your advertisements designed to attract the best people?

- [?] Are you content with the response you get to advertisements?

- [?] Does your organization respond well to applicants' first enquiries?

- [?] Are you satisfied with the way in which your organization trawls through the applicants and selects those for further consideration?

- [?] Does your method for selecting the shortlist guarantee that you see those applicants with the best potential?

- [?] Are you satisfied with the quality of your final decisions in recruitment?

5

Selection processes

▶ Be clear about the purpose of selection

▶ Be careful if you use selection tests

▶ You might find trainability tests useful for some jobs

▶ Explore candidates' relevant previous experience

▶ Prepare interview procedures and interviewers with great care

▶ Take care to ensure that your procedures are open and fair, and are seen as such

Purpose of selection

Selection processes are used both at the recruitment stage and for promotion within the company. The main difference is that when selecting internal candidates there is usually more information available and it is probably more reliable.

On a visit to an engineering company in the UK Midlands some years ago, a consultant interviewed the chief engineer. In answer to a question about recruitment of graduate engineers, the chief engineer stated categorically that under no circumstances would he recruit a woman. The consultant asked the reason for this policy. The engineer replied that when he lifted a heavy piece of machinery he wanted a strong man at the other end to help him. The consultant then asked whether the engineer checked on the physical strength of his male applicants. He did not. He had no logical reason for this prejudice.

The early stages in the recruitment process are described in Chapter 4. The stages may be summarized as follows:

- identifying the post(s) to be filled;

- advertising for suitable candidates;

- selecting candidates for shortlisting; and

- making the final decision.

Consider the purpose of the selection. Are you recruiting or promoting someone to fill a particular job vacancy or a person who can perform a range of tasks appropriate to a group of staff?

One of the characteristics of modern organizations is that as information becomes more distributed, so decisions become more dispersed and delegated to individuals and teams of people at all levels in the organization. The strength of teamwork lies in the ability of a diverse group of people to tackle difficult problems and challenges. In seeking to manage diversity you have the opportunity to enable people to make a contribution to the success of the enterprise. Remember that you cannot make a good team out of a group of identical people. Your selection procedures must enable you to recruit a diversity of people into the group, while maintaining the standard in terms of ability.

Selection tests

In this chapter we want to concentrate on the tests that can be used and on interview procedures. A wide range of intelligence and psychological tests has been devised to aid in the selection of candidates for employment and promotion. There are also trainability tests, simulation exercises and tests of skill. In some cases a 'battery' of tests is used, checking the ability of the candidate to perform a range of tasks.

Some people have an aptitude for learning particular subjects or skills such as languages or working with machines or numbers. There are tests for aptitudes covering, for example, mechanical ability, clerical, numerical and spatial skills, and for artistic and creative ability. Manual dexterity takes many forms and it is generally better to devise tests that measure the ability to be used (see 'Trainability tests' below) rather than general dexterity tests. Such tests can work well for some semi-skilled jobs.

There are four fundamental issues to be considered in using each test:

● How close is the correlation between the results of the test and the ability to perform the roles and responsibilities envisaged?

● How thoroughly have the tests been validated in use with the type of people being examined?

● What feedback will those who administer and assess the results give to those who take the test?

● Does the test, as administered and used, have face validity with the people involved? That is, does the test appear to be valid to the people involved, many of whom will not be experts in selection methods?

Many jobs can be undertaken in a number of ways, especially jobs at a managerial level. Accordingly, two people with different skill mixes may each be able to succeed in the job although they will do it in different ways, for example, varying the balance of the time on different tasks and the way they delegate. As jobs are constantly changing it is unwise to seek too close a match between tests and performance. Interpretation of results, particularly when looking at personality, require a thorough knowledge of psychology, familiarity with the test, and the relevance of the test to the position under consideration – a tall order.

> **Do the test results relate to job performance?**

Even larger pitfalls await the unwary in using tests designed for one population (particularly in terms of language and culture) on people who have a different first language and cultural background. The introduction of culture and gender bias is all too easy.

If you do decide that your selection process would be improved by using selected tests it is worthwhile keeping a record over time to see if you can discern any correlations. This will be difficult if the jobs keep changing, but if you have chosen to select for a group of posts or a level in the hierarchy rather than a specific job, such data can prove valuable. You may wish to set simple threshholds where you consider, for example, that basic levels of literacy and numeracy are required for specific jobs. Even here you must be wary of setting targets higher than necessary as this can discriminate against people with a different first language – people who with a bit more experience and exposure to your company's culture could make a valuable contribution.

People who are asked to take psychological tests are owed feedback on their results. This must be done in a sensitive and constructive manner. It is a counselling and coaching exercise. If a person has a character trait that debars him from a certain kind of work, he needs to know, and to be made to think of alternative avenues for his talent. A person who is accepted may well have characteristics that she needs to take into account as she develops her abilities.

People need to understand the reason behind tests and to be convinced that these represent a fair, rational and unbiased tool of selection. Some people will be daunted by the very thought of tests, and if they have not taken anything of this kind before, you should consider running preparatory tests so that candidates will not fear the procedures involved. This is quite feasible if you are using these tests to select people for promotion. If your employees see the tests as unfair and choosing the 'wrong' people, it will damage morale and could hinder the effectiveness of your organization. There is a mystique around psychological tests, and a suspicion surrounds some of the simulation exercises such as assessment centres. If you use these you must do all in your power to improve their face validity – the belief that they are fair and reasonable.

> **People who are asked to take psychological tests are owed feedback on their results**

Do remember that people who experience the education and training system in one country may well have absorbed much of the culture of that country. Such people may not fare so well in your tests if there is – as there will often be – some cultural bias in the test material.

Simulation exercises

Simulation exercises have been used for a very long time and where they are well designed and executed they have proved a valuable aid in the selection of people for a particular range of tasks. Often such exercises may take two to five days, with participants being asked to perform a range of tasks of the type they will encounter in the jobs being considered, for example civil service administration or sales management. This may involve, for instance, examining case histories or dossiers, identifying key points, making recommendations for action, composing documents (requests, replies, reports), conducting negotiations or investigations, conducting interviews or manipulating financial or other numerical data. The simulations will often involve interactions with other participants or with people who will 'act out' parts such as interviewees. The way people behave under these circumstances, including the way they interact with each other, may be used to try to predict how they will perform in the type of job envisaged.

Those who conduct this type of exercise must be thoroughly conversant with the techniques employed, especially the method of observation and recording, and the relevance of the results to the jobs. Again there is a need to recognize differences in the way people will tackle jobs and the way people of different cultural backgrounds will react to situations.

Trainability tests

Tests can be designed to identify people who can benefit from training. The applicant is taught how to make a simple work-piece or how to operate a part of a process and is observed throughout the procedure and assessed while performing the task. It is essential to ensure that the work-piece or process chosen incorporates crucial aspects of the job and elements that are known to be difficult for some trainees to grasp. At the instructional stage the trainee is encouraged to ask questions and seek help as required. These tests have been used for a number of manual tasks and trades.

> ▶ Tests can be designed to identify people who can benefit from training

These tests may be included in the selection process where successful applicants will be expected to accept training. The tests have proved of value where there are a number of jobs to be filled requiring, for example, specific manual operations requiring a high degree of dexterity. As with most tests, the cost of preparing the tests and checking on their validity is high, and thus the procedures are justified only where the skills are highly critical, or where the numbers of employees involved will be large.

Previous experience

It is not always easy to determine the relevance of a candidate's previous experience. Information regarding a new recruit is normally obtained from the application form and from references. You can check up on qualifications in most cases, and you should always do this before confirming an appointment. It is always difficult to judge the worth of qualifications received in other countries. There are now schemes to help you judge the worth of educational qualifications, and within the European Community there are procedures based on Directives that should help you determine the value of vocational qualifications. These procedures are helpful in some cases, but less so in many occupations where practice varies markedly from one country to another and where the training procedures are very different.

In dealing with higher-level qualifications it often helps to know something of the reputation of the awarding institution. But even in the sciences, the content of courses will vary markedly from one university to another and if you are interested in particular subject areas you may need to question the candidate closely to find the subject areas covered.

Judgements based on references are particularly difficult. One of the key issues is the extent to which you can rely on the individual providing the information – and his prejudices. A reference that provides factual information about the individual's period of employment and the nature of the job can be helpful.

If you are considering internal candidates for promotion you will probably have on record her performance appraisals and comments from people who have managed her in the past. Such information will be valuable provided the system is used well, with managers trained to prepare these appraisals properly, discuss them thoroughly with the individual, and record them systematically. It is most helpful if you have to hand appraisals or assessments from more than one manager. It sometimes happens that an individual who performs poorly with one manager can shine under the guidance of another.

> ▶ Judgements based on references are particularly difficult

In some cultures the person's perceived worth, based on family or on the educational establishment attended, can influence the decision. To the westerner this may seem illogical and unfair. But the fact is that this is an expectation that can be self-fulfilling. If you are recruiting in such a culture, diplomacy may be needed if you consider, for example, that a younger or a female person should be promoted over an older man.

Interview procedures

In the final analysis, the interview is still the most used method of selection, usually alongside a close examination of the applicant's application form and, in the case of internal applicants, his employment record. This may be supplemented by references and test results. Many of us have experienced interview situations where we feel that we were not given a fair opportunity to present ourselves and our abilities in relation to the opportunity on offer. In managing diversity you must make every effort to see that everybody feels fairly treated.

Most managers are now aware of the importance of asking 'open questions' in interviews. If you ask an individual if he would like to work for your company, he can reply yes or no. If you ask him why he wants to work for your company you give him an opportunity to talk about how he sees the company and the prospect of working for it. If you ask him how he believes he is qualified to do the job on offer, this is an open question, but it assumes that he knows in detail what the job entails and what abilities are needed to do it. Many people who would be quite capable of doing the job may find this question difficult. It is expecting a great deal of the candidate.

Organizations that wish to recruit people without recent experience of work in their industry have found that the questions need to be even more open. You need to ask applicants about experiences they have had and how they have tackled problems that can give you an indication of their potential approach to the job. This means more work for the interviewers in interpreting the replies. Often you then find that candidates have been involved in family or voluntary activities that require practical or organizational skills that demonstrate their talents.

> **Ask people about experiences they have had and how they have tackled problems**

This line of questioning has also been of value to organizations that seek to enhance the promotion prospects of minority groups. This is not preferentially promoting people of a particular group, but seeking to discover talent and the ability to perform within these groups. The idea is not to lower standards but to use selection methods that enable you to spot ability in what may have been untapped sources – perhaps coupled with the developmental programmes mentioned in Chapter 9.

Another point to bear in mind in interviews is that the cultural background may well influence the mode of the replies and the level of eye contact. In some cultures people like to spell out the general situation before moving to the specifics of the question. An interviewer from the UK or the USA might interpret this as 'flannel', but this approach does make sense. Provided the final answer is satisfactory, the interviewer's patience may be rewarded. In some cultures, looking directly at a superior is regarded as a challenge to authority, so you may find the person always averts his eyes when speaking to you. You may regard this as evasion instead of a mark of respect. Interviewers need to be alert to these factors.

If you are to avoid discrimination in the interview procedure you should restrict your questioning to areas that are relevant to the job. You must think very clearly about this. In the UK, the USA and many other countries, discrimination on the basis of race, gender or disability is illegal, and in some countries the law is wider still – in the USA for example, it covers age. In general, exemption to this can be allowed only if there is a very good case, for example on the grounds of public decency, or the clear inability (for example of a person with a particular disability) to perform the job. If you are embracing a comprehensive diversity management policy, you will wish to ensure that your interview procedure is demonstrably free of bias.

> **Ensure that all those who conduct selection interviews are well trained**

You must ensure that all those who conduct selection interviews are well trained to avoid questions that might imply selection on the basis of race, nationality, creed, gender, disability, age, family commitments, sexual orientation or lifestyle. You may not wish to exclude from recruitment people with criminal convictions that are not relevant, or carers who may be able to work only on a part-time basis and may need to be called away at short notice. Your interviewers must be careful not to put a question to one candidate that you would not put to every candidate.

A female middle manager in a large organization joined a selection panel for the first time. Of the senior management posts, only about 11 per cent were filled by women. The organization had an equal opportunities policy, ensuring that able women were recruited and nominated for consideration when promotion opportunities arose. The panel, composed of six men and the female middle manager, was selecting external candidates. On the first day it so happened that all the candidates were women. On the second day, all the candidates were men. The female manager noticed that on average the men were being graded more highly than the women, although she could see no justification for the higher marks. When she raised this with her colleagues on the selection panel, she was told that the men had each expanded on the points raised and thus demonstrated their breadth of knowledge. But the woman manager pointed out that the women had merely answered the questions put in a succinct and precise fashion. Indeed, ▶

▶ because of this precision the women had answered many more questions than the male candidates in the same time, and had, in fact, demonstrated as much, if not more, knowledge than the men on each topic. The panel agreed to review the marks awarded and as a result the average mark finally awarded for the women was, in fact, equal to that of the men.

Interviews provide the opportunity for you to judge applicants and their suitability to do a good job for your organization. But they also provide an opportunity for the applicant to make a judgement about whether or not he would really like to work for your company and whether he feels that he could do a decent job for you. The interview procedure should, therefore, allow the applicant time for questions. You may well find these questions instructive, both in what they tell you about the applicant and in what they tell you about his perception of the company and the job. You must be prepared to field questions about how the firm deals with harassment or bullying, and how people that are different in some way are treated by fellow workers.

For recruitment, candidates often face a one-to-one interview with a personnel officer, to be followed by a one-to-one interview with the potential line manager. Although the one-to-one interview is comparatively low key and non-threatening, there is a very real possibility of bias. If there is a danger that the candidate will fear discrimination, every effort must be made to allay that fear, and the behaviour and demeanour of the inter-viewers is crucial. Often the better system is to have two people at the final interview, provided the role of each person during the session is defined and adhered to throughout.

The results of the interview must be recorded together with the reasons for the appointment, or non-appointment, clearly laid out. In many countries this is a legal requirement if you wish to avoid any claim for unfair treatment. For internal promotions, you may also want to decide at the time just what you will tell unsuccessful candidates. Feedback from the selection process can be a fruitful basis for growth and development. If the candidate does not have any prospect of promotion, then guidance into an alternative career path might be helpful.

It must be emphasized that in some cultures the desire for constant promotion and the ascent up the corporate ladder are not as pronounced as they appear to be in the UK and the USA. As organizations become flatter the need for incremental steps up the corporate ladder will be less significant. People in the future are more likely to grow with the job, and be prepared to move laterally for more experience and job enrichment. These factors emphasize the need to recruit on a broader basis than simple job descriptions.

In conducting interviews it is common practice to ask some light-hearted questions unrelated to the matter in hand to put the interviewee at ease. In some cultures it is regarded as essential to get to know the person as a person before doing any business with them, so this stage may be particularly important to some people, and may involve the interviewers talking about themselves and their organization as well as listening to the interviewee.

Be seen as fair

If you are managing a diverse workforce within a diverse population, not only must your selection procedures be fair both for recruitment and promotion, they must be seen to be fair. Except at senior levels, you should avoid the practice of deciding on managerial appointments behind closed doors, with the process shrouded in mystery. For all appointments, the criteria for selection and the procedures to be used must be open and above board. At the end of the day most people must be able to say: 'That appointment was fair.'

> ▶ Criteria for selection and the procedures to be used must be open and above board

You may be tempted to appoint people to achieve certain targets, such as equal numbers of women or the 'right' proportion of black people or disabled people. Don't. Always promote the people who can do the job. To get the balance right, use other means, for example more widespread advertising for jobs, attention to avoiding discrimination in the recruitment process, or providing mentor help for disadvantaged people.

Progress checklist

[?] Have you thought about how the organization will develop and the roles and responsibilities people are likely to face in the future?

[?] Are your selection procedures geared to a flexible future?

[?] Have you chosen selection tests with care and trained people to conduct them properly?

[?] Do you consider that trainability tests have any part to play in selection procedures?

[?] Are your procedures for considering a candidate's previous experience effective?

[?] Have you taken the trouble to ensure that your procedures are seen as fair?

6

Conditions of service

▶ Incorporate diversity into your terms and conditions of service

▶ Update your equal opportunity policies

▶ Check out your recruitment, training and communications practices

▶ Deal with discrimination, bullying and harassment

▶ Make your policies people friendly

▶ Examine policies on health and safety, security and compliance issues

▶ Consider a code of conduct for all employees

The terms and conditions of service you require of your employees may need to be reviewed as you enhance your organization's diversity management. Many organizations publish their terms and conditions of employment in a company handbook and some post them on the company's intranet. The handbook is normally loose-leaf, allowing for pages to be replaced as policies are developed.

There are a number of areas where conditions of service impact on diversity. Often there is a need to begin by setting out some key definitions. Define the employer, the status of employees and the person who is regarded as the manager for the purposes of supervision, grievance and discipline procedures. Key topics include:

● diversity management, including equal opportunities;

● internal recruitment, external recruitment, probationary period;

- salary, hours of work, flexible hours and overtime;
- training and development;
- communication and consultation procedures;
- grievance, discipline and dismissal procedures, absence/lateness procedures;
- other occupations, termination of employment, maternity rights;
- people-friendly conditions, holidays and leave of absence;
- retirement and disability benefits;
- health and safety.

Hours of work and benefit packages are discussed below under 'People-friendly policies'. *See also* Chapters 11 and 12.

Diversity management and equal opportunities

Many organizations describe their equal opportunity policies and practices in detail and extracts are provided below. Some companies make explicit their policies on diversity, and may indicate the behaviour they expect of their employees in supporting such policies. Where appropriate, an organization may make specific reference to its aim to reflect within the diversity of its employees the make-up of the communities it serves. Organizations might also refer to the wider aim of treating their customers, suppliers and shareholders with the same respect as their employees. These policies are normally backed up by procedures at each stage in the recruitment and employment process: breach of the policy may, in some cases, be a specific disciplinary matter.

Extracts from diversity and equal opportunity policies

It is the Company's policy to offer equal opportunity to all in its employment and its policies and procedures take this into account. All employees must share the responsibility of ensuring equal opportunity by not discriminating on the grounds of sex, marital status, disability, creed, colour, race or ethnic origin. The Company has made and will continue to make every effort to retain and assist any of its employees that become disabled and to help with their rehabilitation. *(Schroders plc)*

Equality of opportunity for all sections of our community and workforce is an essential value for this Council. This means recognizing the inequalities which people suffer and taking action to reduce them. Everyone has a role to play in ensuring fairness towards colleagues and the community we serve. *(Lewisham Council, London)*

It is BT's policy that: no job applicant or employee receives less favourable treatment in any aspect of employment on racial grounds or on the grounds of gender, religion, disability, marital status, age or sexual orientation, gender status or caring responsibilities or be disadvantaged by conditions or requirements which cannot be shown to be justifiable.

There must be no unlawful discrimination, direct, indirect or institutional, against any eligible person whether in recruitment, selection, training, promotion or in any aspect of employment. Harassment of any form at work is also a form of discrimination and will be treated as such under the terms of this policy. No form of harassment or bullying, including derogatory remarks at work, will be tolerated.

Positive measures will be taken to encourage the recruitment and employment of any underrepresented minority group. Our goal is to reflect the diversity of all the communities within which we operate and to carefully monitor our progression toward this goal.

All BT people have an obligation to uphold this policy and disciplinary action will be considered where deliberate breach takes place. This could also be unlawful. *(BT plc)*

Honda is an equal opportunities employer. In order to promote an environment within which the company can call upon the widest possible range of knowledge, skill and experience, as well as ensuring compliance with the relevant legislation and codes of practice, we are committed to achieving and maintaining a workforce which represents the population within our recruitment area in terms of race or colour, nationality, ethnic origins, sex or marital status and disability. *(Honda, UK)*

SB operates in diverse cultures, environments and communities. These communities embrace employees, potential employees, customers, suppliers and shareholders. Our aim is to recognize and reflect these differences in our workforce and business environment. The SB definition of Equality and Diversity is 'Creating an environment where the potential of the skills and expertise of all our employees is realized through recognizing and valuing differences in people'. *(SmithKline Beecham)*

It is the policy of the Company to treat job applicants and employees in the same way, irrespective of sex, sexual orientation, marital status, age, colour, race, nationality, religion, ethnic origin or disability throughout its operations and to establish the means by which this policy is to be achieved. *(BAE Systems)*

Some organizations include within the conditions of service a specific policy in respect of disabled people, promising to give them full, fair and sympathetic consideration in applications for employment, promotion and redeployment. In the event of an employee becoming disabled, every effort will be made to continue employment wherever possible. The British Post

Office is proud to declare itself an equal opportunities employer. Some employers make specific reference to carers (people who look after disabled or infirm relatives at home) and others refer to the fact that they will consider for employment people with criminal convictions where, in the opinion of the employer, the offence is not relevant to employment in the organization.

Whereas some organizations see diversity in terms of compliance with the law, others go beyond this and seek to engender a positive culture of respect for every individual. SmithKline Beecham literature refers to recognizing and valuing diversity. Reuters has undertaken a worldwide imaginative training programme for all its managers, reinforcing the company's equal employment opportunity policy and its approach to respect for the individual while reminding them of the local legislation relating to diversity issues.

Hickson and Welch, a chemical manufacturer based in Castleford, Yorkshire, employs about 400 people. It has a long history of collaboration with the Transport and General Workers' Union, and its Human Resources Director, Les Shaw, was formerly the union convenor. For a period, Mr Shaw occupied the joint role of personnel officer and trade union convenor. The company has a policy agreed in partnership with the T&G that includes a wide-ranging equal opportunities policy. This amounts to a diversity policy. The managing director, John Markham, believes that its success in a highly competitive world depends on the company's employees and the development of their skills and abilities. The equal opportunity policy includes the following: 'There will be no discrimination on grounds of sex, marital status, colour, disability or age in assessing the suitability of any one individual for employment. The principle will apply to recruitment, training, promotion, disciplinary actions, transfer and all other benefits and terms and conditions of employment.'

Recruitment, training and communications

Recruitment policies and procedures need to take fully into account the organization's approach to diversity (*see* Chapter 4). Training and development is an ongoing process and should be designed to enable people to perform their tasks and to enable those with the requisite ability to prepare themselves for more demanding tasks and, where appropriate, for promotion (*see* Chapter 9). The organization may need to impress upon managers the need to provide extra help, where this is needed, for people with disabilities.

When setting up communication and consultation procedures (Chapter 7), ensure that all sections of the workforce can participate, for example those people who work atypical hours, or who have caring responsibilities or a disability.

Grievance, discipline and discrimination

Grievance procedures must allow people to make complaints about discrimination, bullying or harassment without fear of reprisals (unless the complaint can be shown to be malicious). Most grievance procedures invite the employee who has a problem or difficulty connected with work to talk it over with his immediate manager at the outset. Unfortunately, it may be the manager who is the cause of the problem. Thus organizations need to set up alternative routes for employees to raise such matters. Often this involves an equal opportunities adviser, someone in the human resources department, or a mediator (see below).

The procedures need to be swift, but fair, and must allow the complainant to raise the matter with higher levels of management as appropriate. At any stage the matter can be referred back to an earlier part of the process, de-escalating the seriousness of the incident if this is likely to bring about a resolution of the problem. In cases of harassment or discrimination of one employee by another, the aim must be to bring about a cessation of the offending action and hopefully a reconciliation between the parties concerned and the building of an effective, cordial working relationship.

Increasingly, organizations are using a system of '**mediators**' to facilitate this process, hopefully resolving problems before they become official complaints. Members of staff volunteer and those who prove suitable are trained for this mediation role. This is in addition to their normal work. An employee who feels aggrieved can appeal to a mediator who will talk to the parties involved and seek to deal with the problem without recourse to the official grievance or discipline procedures. Of course, if the bully does not respond to mediation, the matter can be referred to management for disciplinary action – provided this is included in the terms and conditions of service. Mediation is not used in cases of serious allegations of misconduct. The discipline procedure should provide for action if, ultimately, a member of staff persists in discriminatory, bullying or harassing behaviour. In extreme cases this can lead to suspension or even dismissal. Discipline procedures can be initiated immediately if the incident is serious enough. To be effective, the mediator must be acceptable to both parties involved.

Most people want some feedback on how they are seen by management in the performance of their jobs. The way that you do this task, and the use you make of the results, will have a profound effect on morale and the effectiveness of the workforce. Sensitivity in dealing with people who suffer any form of disadvantage is essential.

Depending on the country in question, the grounds on which an employee can claim discrimination can include gender, marital status, race, religion, political beliefs, family status or responsibilities, pregnancy or potential pregnancy, disability (both physical and intellectual), parenthood, age, sexual preference, union membership or non-membership.

Some organizations have specific policies and procedures to deal with bullying and harassment. A typical policy might read: 'We seek to create a work climate that values difference, where harassment, intimidation and offensive behaviour is unacceptable, and individuals are confident in resolving any such issue without fear of ridicule or reprisal.'

To eliminate harassment requires more than issuing a definition. The term needs to be explained and illustrated to avoid any ambiguity. Harassment can be any unwanted and offensive behaviour by one individual towards another that makes the recipient feel offended, humiliated, threatened or patronized. The impact of such behaviour varies, so that what would be offensive to one person would be regarded as acceptable to another. It may also vary with the circumstances. It is usual to say that harassment has occurred if this is the impact perceived by the recipient. The intention of the alleged perpetrator is not the issue. Often it is the persistence of such behaviour that causes distress, but one incident can be serious enough to constitute harassment.

> ▶ **Increasingly, organizations are using a system of 'mediators'**

The way a group behaves under normal circumstances may result in an unwelcoming environment for a newcomer, particularly if that newcomer is in some way different. Organizations need to cultivate a positive attitude towards diversity and not just prohibit discrimination. People must be encouraged to go beyond tolerance to acceptance of the worth of people who are, in some way, different to themselves. Bullying is considered to be a particular form of harassment.

Many organizations now keep a careful record of all incidents of harassment, bullying or other forms of discrimination. Monitoring can indicate individuals or areas of the company where action needs to be taken.

If these activities are not kept in check, people will leave the organization and may seek legal redress. Companies that conduct effective exit interviews have found that sometimes people leave because of harassment rather than raise the matter under the grievance procedure.

There may be specific forms of harassment in your organization. In some cases it may have been in place for many years and the behaviour is regarded as 'normal'. Newcomers are expected to put up with the behaviour.

Harassment can create an intimidating, hostile or offensive working environment, adversely affecting work performance and employment prospects, and can reflect on the integrity and standing of the organization. Harassment can be concerned with a person's race, gender, ethnic origin, nationality, marital status, pregnancy, disability, age, family responsibility, family status, sexual orientation, religious or political conviction. It may also be concerned with a person's appearance (including obesity), speech or accent.

Examples of harassing or discriminatory behaviour in general can include:

- graffiti – for example, sexual or racial
- jokes or ridicule about the person's race, gender, physical attributes, etc
- derogative name calling
- ostracism
- swearing at someone
- using physical presence to intimidate
- unwarranted physical contact.

Sexual harassment is a specific category of harassment and as such it may be recognized in law, for example in the USA, where it is defined as 'unwelcome sexual advances, requests for sexual favours, and other verbal or physical conduct of a sexual nature'. Sexual harassment may take the form of an action that is accompanied by an employment threat or benefit, such as the suggestion that advancement is dependent on sexual favours. Alternatively, sexual harassment may take the form of creating a hostile environment, for example by the exhibition of pornographic material or sexual jokes. Whether or not the items on the following list constitute sexual harassment will depend on the circumstances, but the likelihood is that they will, and they should be avoided:

- posters, pictures, calendars, cartoons, graffiti or messages of an erotic or sexually explicit nature displayed on notice boards or left in full view on desks;

- electronic mail messages, voice mail messages, screen savers, offensive telephone calls or faxes of an erotic or sexually explicit nature, or making improper suggestions;

- unwarranted and unwanted physical contact – patting, pinching, fondling, attempts at kissing or deliberately brushing against another person's body;

- leering or staring at another person's body;

- sexist jokes or comments, tales of sexual prowess;

- sexual innuendo, provocative remarks, suggestive or derogatory remarks about a person's physical appearance;

- persistent requests for dates after refusal;

- requests for sexual favours, gestures or body movements of a sexual or intimidating nature;

- intrusive inquiries into a person's private life, sexuality or appearance.

Racial harassment is another specific form of harassment, often based on stereotypical and inaccurate assumptions about people from ethnic minority groups. It can be verbal, non-verbal or physical. It may consist of offensive gestures or facial expressions, publications, letters, memoranda or graffiti. Racist jokes, ridicule, comments, abuse and nicknames can be involved. It may degenerate into threatening behaviour, verbal threats, jostling or assault.

> ▶ Sexual harassment may take the form of creating a hostile environment

People-friendly policies

A number of conditions of service will impact directly on people's personal lives outside of work. We use the phrase 'people-friendly policies' to embrace the whole issue of work-life balance (Chapter 12). Many families now have only one adult member, and in others there are elderly or infirm relatives who need regular care and attention at home.

One of the unfortunate developments in some countries is the tendency for people to work very long hours, or at least to spend a lot of time in the workplace. Some companies seem to have created a culture of long atten-dance hours such that going home on time is viewed as an indication of lack of commitment. Junior executives, in particular, sometimes seem to think that staying late is the way to get noticed. Long hours deprive parents of the opportunity to see their children and participate fully in family life.

Organizations are just beginning to recognize that long hours day after day, week after week, month after month actually reduce the effectiveness of most people, often leading to stress-related illnesses. If the operation must be manned for long periods of time, flexible attendance patterns are a much better way of covering the required hours so that individuals are not subjected to such pressures. Men as well as women want to spend time with their families and you should extend to male employees the same consider-ation that you extend to female employees. Neither should be required to work excessive, unsocial hours over long periods.

Some organizations offer a range of benefit packages tailored to individuals. These might include atypical leave patterns or working hours,

> ▶ Some organizations offer a range of benefit packages tailored to individuals

sabbaticals, stock options, therapy, insurance arrangements, tax advice, financial provision for children and school fees. In some very well paid jobs, the emphasis is no longer on salary but on provision for the quality of life. Such flexibility provides an opportunity for the organization to meet the range of needs of a diverse workforce. The organization may also provide, usually on a wider basis, catering facilities and medical care, loans and salary advances and season ticket assistance, personal accident insurance, a company car scheme and a share ownership scheme. Benefits can also include the ability to buy goods at discounted prices and cheap loans to help employees to buy their own homes. You must ensure that all the relevant tax laws are observed, and that all your employees have equal access to these benefits.

Policies on holidays should be flexible enough to cope with the religious holidays of people of diverse faiths. For example, the company may endeavour to allow the individual time off to observe religious holidays, but count such holidays against the annual leave entitlement. If there is a policy on compas-sionate leave, a diversity policy would not distinguish between married and unmarried partners in stable relationships, or between single-sex and male/female relationships. There is usually a provision for paid leave if a close relative dies, and the same conditions should apply. People who have come to live and work in the UK often have relatives and friends in other countries, particularly the Caribbean and the Indian sub-continent. They may want to take extended leave so that they can travel to spend time with these people. It should be possible for your leave allocation system to cope with this, for example by allowing people to accumulate their leave allocation.

Some organizations grant special leave for study, medical or dental appointments, for jury service, for duties in connection with a court of law or to deal with domestic problems. In each case care must be taken to avoid discrimination. Many organizations operate schemes to help people who become disabled or suffer from long-term illnesses. The provision may exclude people who become disabled through engaging in hazardous pursuits in their own time. In some cases the benefit will be paid to the spouse if the employee dies.

Many organizations operate a pension scheme to which the employee may contribute. A few offer non-contributory pension schemes. When the employee dies there is often a provision for the spouse. In relation to both the disability benefit and the retirement benefit, the diversity definition of a spouse would not distinguish between married and unmarried partners in stable relationships, or between single-sex and male/female relationships.

Health and safety, security and compliance

Health and safety policies typically cover the relevant legislation, fire evacuation procedures, bomb threats (if relevant), first-aid arrangements, lifts, occupational health matters, visual display units, substance abuse, smoking and Aids/hepatitis B. As mentioned elsewhere, special arrangements may be necessary for people with language problems or those who suffer from a disability.

Security matters often include specific procedures related to company property, visitors, unauthorized personnel, access to company premises (including the use of entry codes and identity cards, and restricted areas), personal property and security guards. Reference is often made to the use and misuse of computers, and publicity matters.

Most organizations now have to comply with a complex range of laws and regulations. Organizations in industries such as finance and medicines often set up departments and procedures to ensure that they comply with all relevant regulations in each country where they operate or provide goods and services. Some have included compliance with diversity matters within this remit.

The investment management activities of Schroders plc operate through offices in 33 countries. In common with all organizations that operate within the financial sector, there is a strong adherence to compliance requirements. The organization operates through mixed multinational teams with currently 50 people on secondment across countries. Virtually everyone speaks English within the industry, but Japan can sometimes present language difficulties. Because senior people travel a great deal, much of the internal business is conducted by telephone and video conferencing.

Policy statements on discrimination, harassment, compliance and disabled people are all in the staff handbook and on the intranet. Exit interviews are regularly conducted on a worldwide basis and can give valuable indications of potential problems on the people management side. Any problems that arise are investigated thoroughly and action taken, for example to deal with harassment or discrimination. Global labour turnover data is analyzed by age and gender. The company's policies, for example for an employee who becomes disabled, apply to everybody, irrespective of race, throughout the world.

The organization has moved beyond family-friendly policies and now talks in terms of life-friendly policies, helping people to tailor-make arrangements that they need to lead fulfilling lives. Managing diversity is seen as giving people the opportunity to balance their lives with their business. Top management at Schroders see every employee as an 'ambassador', and encourage every employee to develop his or her potential.

Codes of conduct

Some organizations that are serious about diversity management have, after extensive consultation with employees, drawn up codes of conduct. Such a code may deal with matters outside diversity, and cover many aspects of behaviour at work that the company and the employees would wish to encourage. In some cases these codes may be related to specific diversity issues such as harassment.

Quotes from codes of conduct:

'**Employees are expected** to behave at all times in a reasonable and proper way towards fellow employees, the Company, its suppliers, distributors and customers.' *(Honda)*

'**The Company strives** to maintain the highest standard of business conduct. To ensure honesty and fairness in dealing with staff, customers, suppliers, competitors and government you should avoid any activity or interest that might reflect unfavourably on your own or the Company's integrity. The Code of Conduct outlines the responsibilities of all the Company's employees.' *(Reuters)*

Progress checklist

☐ How recently and thoroughly have you reviewed your terms and conditions of employment to ensure conformity with diversity management?

☐ Do you have a specific equal opportunities policy? What does it cover?

☐ Are your recruitment and training practices consistent with your diversity policy?

☐ Do you have effective measures to deal with discrimination, harassment and bullying? Do these procedures give people access to redress without fear of reprisals?

☐ To what extent do your conditions of service support people-friendly policies that take into account modern family life and lifestyles?

☐ Have you considered the idea of a code of conduct for employees, drawn up in discussion with them?

☐ If you negotiate with a trade union, does your agreement cover diversity issues?

7

Communication channels

▶ Recognize effective communications as a two-way process

▶ Be wary of the image you convey by external communications

▶ Manage knowledge and information within your organization

▶ Generate feedback from employees

▶ Encourage communications across the organization

Two-way communication

We all know that effective communications are essential for success, whether it is in terms of advertising your products and services or letting people in your organization know just what it is they need to do. But in both cases it needs to become a two-way process. You need to know what your customers want. And you should be interested in what your own people have to say about the products and services, and the way they are produced. It also makes sense to listen to your other business contacts, be they the banker, investor, supplier – or government!

▶ **Ensure that communications are effective at achieving their goals**

Yet over and over again we find organizations which do not listen carefully to their customers and business contacts, and senior managers who do not listen to their employees. In both cases this behaviour leads to problems and it has been the downfall of more than one enterprise. The problems become more acute when your customers and your employees are diverse.

Particular problems arise over the language you use and the cultures involved, and this is discussed in Chapter 13. Problems can also arise when people have hearing, seeing or comprehension difficulties (*see* Chapter 14). As part of the management of diversity it makes sense to take an overview of your communications practices and to check them out against these potential problems to ensure their effectiveness.

External communications

What is your impression of the way that customers, potential employees and the public at large perceive your organization? How do your shareholders see the company? Is the organization seen as an equal opportunity employer? Would a disabled person expect to receive a sympathetic response to an application for employment? Would a woman applying for a post in say engineering or production management expect to be interviewed fairly and treated with respect by all managers and colleagues? Would a black youth expect to be accepted in your organization? How do you know?

These questions need to be addressed. Review each avenue of communications to see what message is being put across – and then check out what message is being received. It may not be the same! Your organization gives out messages when:

● it places a label on a product or a logo to identify a service;

● it places an advertisement in a local or national newspaper;

● an event relating to the organization is reported in the local newspaper with a photograph;

● you produce promotional literature, for example leaflets to advertise your products and services;

● you second a member of staff to some charitable endeavour;

● one of your senior people appears in a radio or television programme;

● your organization appears in one of the docu-soaps or an exposé.

The list is almost endless. The important point to recognize is that quite apart from the external messages that you can control, there are others in control of the media. For example, newspaper and television editors and reporters can misunderstand, distort, misrepresent or quote out of context information about your organization. You must be aware of this possibility. There is no point in having a sound policy and, in theory, sound practices in place if a senior manager clearly demonstrates his racial or gender prejudice, for example, when interviewed by the media. The solution is not to train senior managers to deal with awkward questions but to ensure that all your senior people and potential spokespeople are at one with you on the issues of diversity. This is one of the reasons we stress the need for a supportive culture, not just as set of policies and prescribed procedures.

Knowledge management

The way people communicate with each other in organizations is very telling. In today's fast-moving world there is no time for organizations where internal communications are slow or ineffective. Nowadays, information is one of the four key factors of production, alongside money, technology and people. Virtually every organization has access to the same information 'out there'. The crucial issue is how your people manage the information you have both in-house and what is available externally.

You may need to pay more attention to ensure effective communications within a diverse workforce. Effective internal communications, where people feel informed and involved, not only improve morale, but are good for business. There is now plenty of evidence to support the notion that if you can get all your people thinking about the business and working to improve it, the results transfer into the bottom line – in terms of higher cost-effectiveness, better products and services, and better customer care. Knowledge management implies more than just shunting information around. It means ensuring that people have enough training and understanding to discriminate between useful and useless information. It implies that when people acquire knowledge they know whether this could be valuable to other people in the organization. It assumes that they have the means to pass this information on to others who will be pleased to get it.

In most organizations the traditional oral and written methods must be augmented, to an extent, by digital technology. All of these methods must be made user-friendly to a diverse population. It is not enough to provide information for employees, whether this is by newsletter, notice board, web pages or video links. They must be helped to learn how to access this, how to understand it and how to use much of it to improve the way they work and get results. Above all they must learn how to filter out the 'noise' – all the unwanted data that can so easily clog up the system.

Management needs to bear in mind that in a diverse workforce there will be people who are working part-time or atypical hours, and people with visual, hearing or comprehension problems. Don't forget the night shift! There may also be people for whom English is not the first language. When an important announcement is made, for example, special measures may be required to ensure that all these people get the same message in clear, comprehensible language at approximately the same time.

To many people the written word and the images that one can see in printed and computer-presented material lack the ring of truth when you need to build trust. If you want to bring about a culture change, people want to see the whites of your eyes. You need to hold face-to-face meetings with people. You will need to convince people that you are actually interested in what they have to say and that you are prepared to change your opinions in the light of their statements. This is particularly important when you are seeking to deal with some of the more sensitive issues associated with diversity, such as gender preferences.

> **▶ Don't forget the night shift!**

Employee feedback

For the day-to-day feedback on how people see what is going on within the organization, the normal mechanisms of briefing groups and employee representative discussions with management can be effective. Where there is an effective, responsible trade union, it makes sense to support the union representative and to channel many matters through her, although this does not preclude management from talking directly to the workforce on occasion to ensure that the message is getting through, and seeking opinions through surveys and focus groups.

Supporting the trade union officer assumes that she has taken the trouble to ensure she is able to represent the views of all sections of the workforce, including men and women, ethnic minorities, young and old, gays, lesbians and heterosexuals, carers and people with disabilities.

In organizations where no trade union is recognized it may still be possible to organize elections for individuals to represent groups of employees. More than 40 years ago there were works councils in the UK, where representatives were able to meet and talk to management about the concerns of groups of people. However, as they generally had no power, they proved effective only insofar as management allowed them to be. The works councils set up under the European Community rules appear to operate at a higher level and may well have an influence on diversity issues.

Many organizations have decided to set up particular mechanisms to help employees to raise their concerns. You must decide how you will tackle this issue of getting feedback from people about diversity. Some of the methods used include:

- **special interest groups,** for example for black people, or for lesbian and gay people, where they can meet for mutual support and draw attention to practices that need to be changed in the organization;

- **networks,** for example for disabled people within the organization, with a representative to voice their concerns to management, or perhaps a newsletter on paper or information posted on the intranet;

- **focus groups,** where people from different backgrounds can share their perceptions about the organization and give feedback to management on how matters can be improved.

- **a champion,** an individual who knows about the problems faced by a particular group, who can keep in touch with members of the group and have access to management at a high level to initiate change;

- **impartial contact,** a member of staff, or even someone outside the organization in some cases, to whom an individual can go with a problem that she feels unable to raise within the organization. The impartial person should know enough about the organization to find a way to deal effectively with the problem;

- **employee surveys** have also been employed, using paper and pencil methods, the intranet, interviews or discussion groups (*see* Chapter 3);

- **exit interviews** may be leaving it too late as far as the leaver is concerned, but many organizations have found that, properly conducted, they give another insight into the way people feel they are treated within the firm.

Each of these mechanisms has been used to deal with the particular problems that the organization faces. The 'impartial person' may be needed in extreme cases where the normal channels of communication – the line manager, the personnel officer, the equal opportunities adviser – are not trusted by some members of the workforce. They may also be needed, for example, by someone who has difficulty communicating and would like a sympathetic interpreter to accompany him when he raises some issue such as bullying or unfair treatment.

Where there is an effective trade union and officers trusted by all sections of the workforce, a trade union representative might well perform this function. Unfortunately, trade union officers have not been without prejudice themselves, but many unions have been tackling this problem with considerable success.

Individuals who have a grievance such as bullying, harassment or unfair treatment may be reluctant to raise this for a number of reasons, for example for fear of reprisals, a reluctance to get someone into the discipline procedure and become unpopular, or an unwillingness to be identified as a troublemaker. This is particularly true when the individual feels in the minority. It may be that the behaviour they want to complain about is, and has been, normal practice for some years. Times are changing, but in some organizations the clock has got stuck! It is to deal with such instances that companies have introduced the concept of mediator. The role of the mediators is described in Chapter 6.

Lateral communications

We have so far focused on upward and downward communications. Much of the day-to-day communications within organizations is between people in the same team and the same department, or across departments. For these communications to be effective, especially in physically separate locations, consider the following issues:

● employees need an understanding of how the operation fits together and where their particular activities fit into this overall picture;

● within the teams, there must be a clear understanding of the team's role and goals and a commitment to achieving these for the good of the whole organization. This must be coupled with mutual respect between team members and an ability and a willingness to work together. Recognizing and valuing difference is even more important in a diverse workforce;

- employees need to understand the work of their colleagues in other sections and departments, and to be aware of the impact of their actions on the ability of others to do their work effectively;

- you need employees who are committed to working for the good of the organization, not just for their personal gain or to the advantage of their particular section. For such commitment to be maintained you will need to ensure that the reward systems and the organizational culture support this attitude and behaviour. To do this you will need to understand people's motivation, and to recognize that people from different cultural backgrounds may have different values that need to be taken into account.

All this assumes that people can actually talk to each other or send e-mails. The physical arrangement of the workplace, the availability of telephones, fax machines, computer terminals, all play a part. It will be important to ensure that no section of the workforce is treated unfairly in respect of access to the means of communication.

Progress checklist

- Do you encourage two-way communication throughout your organization, and with your business contacts?

- Are you confident that the policies you have adopted in respect of diversity are being consistently conveyed by all external communications – planned and unplanned?

- Do you have an effective system for managing knowledge in your organization? Are people trained to manage information and encouraged to share it?

- Have you set up systems that enable employees to raise matters of concern? Are you sure these systems work?

- Are you confident that knowledge and information flow quickly and purposefully across your organization?

- Do your policies and practices stress the value of face-to face communication?

8

Induction and initial training

▶ An effective induction process is essential if you are to retain people drawn from a diverse labour force

▶ Prepare a general induction checklist and adapt this for the needs of each individual newcomer

▶ Ensure that someone is in charge of the overall induction process for each newcomer

▶ Health and safety must be instilled at every stage

▶ Each individual will need a personal development plan, although in some cases this may be relatively simple

▶ Be sure your training takes into account key factors in training a diverse workforce

▶ For each newcomer, assign responsibility for a review of progress

Initial experiences

Experience has shown the crucial importance of the induction and initial training process in helping people to acclimatize to the organization – and helping the organization to accept new people. The training of existing staff is even more important (*see* Chapters 8 and 15). It is useful to distinguish between *induction* – the help you give to newcomers to enable them to become members of your organization – and the *initial training* given to enable them to do their new jobs. What happens in the first few days when an individual joins the firm can make a lasting impression on a newcomer. Attitudes and habits form quickly and change slowly.

There is a great deal to learn if the newcomer is to feel at home and to quickly make a contribution to the organization. This problem of settling into the work is particularly difficult if, for any reason, the individual is at a disadvantage. For example, a woman entering a 'man's world' where every other worker is a male – or a man entering a woman's world. The existing group of people will have a number of expectations of each other, and a culture will have developed. The newcomer could feel threatened. In many ways the groundwork will need to be laid in the training and briefing of the existing group, to prepare them to accept someone of the opposite sex, to recognize the potential problems and to be prepared to change some of their practices. This problem is particularly acute when people come from cultures where the roles of men and women are more distinctly differentiated.

> ▶ **The events of the first few days can make a lasting impression on the newcomer**

You will also need to prepare the way for people who are disadvantaged, for example because they have language difficulties or come from an ethnic minority group or are disabled in some way. Again the staff with whom they work may need to be prepared to accept the newcomers. Pay attention to simple matters such as the signs on toilets and exits, and the basic safety precautions that apply to everyone. Will the newcomers be able to read and respond appropriately? Will people who have hearing or mobility difficulties, or who are partially or totally blind, be able to cope?

The induction process

One way to prepare for new employees is to work through the following induction process checklist (*see also* Table 8.1):

● How will the newcomer be received?

● Who will welcome the newcomer?

● What will each newcomer need to know?

● To whom should the newcomer be introduced?

● What will the newcomer need to be shown?

- At what stage should each item of information be given?
- What should be given in written form and what can be spoken?
- Who will provide the information?
- What follow-up will be undertaken?
- Who will be responsible for the follow-up?

Table 8.1 Induction checklist

This should be read in conjunction with the induction process checklist. The list is not intended to be exhaustive and you will need to check this against local regulations and your organization's needs.

	Examples of items of information	Signature
Employment matters	Contract of employment Terms of probationary period, if any Pay rates, methods of payment, payslips Overtime arrangements Holidays, other leave entitlement and arrangements Sickness, absence and certificates Timekeeping and time-recording methods Trade union membership and recognition Grievance and discipline procedures Diversity and equal opportunity policies and how they are applied	
Starting procedures	Documents required (for example, from previous employer, tax forms, work permit, birth certificate) Medical examination, if required Protective clothing, its provision and use, any compulsory requirements to use Introductions to key people	
General information	Toilets, cloakrooms and washrooms Meals, breaks and eating places Welfare facilities and parking Smoking Security Purchases (for example, of the firm's products if appropriate)	

Health and safety	Safe methods of working Good housekeeping and hygiene First-aid arrangements Fire precautions and exits Response to fire or bomb threats Machine safety, tools and equipment Dangerous substances
The organization	History Organization's divisions and sections Products, services and markets
Personal development plan	Initial training arrangements Development opportunities

Decide on who will first meet the newcomer and what programme of activities will be followed on the first day. Ensure that if you have security people at the gate, they are notified to expect the newcomer, and primed to treat the individual with courtesy and respect. In general it is advisable to get a number of matters cleared up straight away, such as the contract hours of work, payment and overtime. Many of these will have been dealt with before the individual starts work, but it is wise to make sure that all these points are properly understood and that all the paperwork is in order. This will often take an hour or two and can be dealt with by human resource people in their offices.

Then the individual will need to be taken to his or her new place of work. The manager and other workers need to be notified about newcomers. A senior person (usually the manager) should be available to meet them. Often a colleague can be deputed to show the newcomer around. As a newcomer, nothing is worse than finding you have nowhere to sit or no place to work, and that nobody has the time to talk to you or show you around. You do not want to meet the boss for the first time by bumping into her in the corridor without knowing who she is. The newcomer should be shown all the key features of the place of work – the toilets and cloakrooms, staff restaurant, first-aid centres, emergency exits and so forth. Care should be taken with people who have disabilities, for example the inability to negotiate stairways, to hear fire sirens, or to read exit signs.

The number of things the newcomer has to learn is surprising. Look at the induction checklist provided. When you have adapted this list to the needs of your organization, you will have to decide when each point is raised with the newcomer and how. Will a number of items be provided in a handbook? Alternatively, will the information be provided on individual sheets and handed out as each topic is introduced? How much of this written information should be explained or emphasized? If the newcomer has problems with language or with written matter, for example, because English (if that is the language used by the company) is not his first language, or because of poor eyesight, you must decide on what action to take.

If you have a large number of employees whose first language is different to that used by the company, it may be worthwhile to produce documentation in their language. One must be careful about translating legal documents such as contracts of employment, however, as the translation may not do justice to the original. It may be necessary in such cases to preface the translation with a disclaimer, stating that the document in the original language is authoritative, but not the translation. If you employ a number of people with eyesight problems it may be useful to produce Braille versions of key documents, or to provide tape-recorded versions. Whatever approach you adopt, try to ensure, as far as possible, that every employee is helped to understand what is required of him, and how he can get access to all the facilities he will require.

> **The number of things the newcomer has to learn is surprising**

You will need to determine when each piece of information is conveyed, and how, and who will convey it. It is wise to produce a written checklist and to give a copy to the individual and to a responsible person who can see that all the points are covered. This will usually be the individual's manager. As an extra precaution you may ask the newcomer to sign off each item on the manager's copy when it has been covered. This signed copy can be lodged in the personnel file. This will ensure that the material has been covered and could be important if the individual is later involved in an accident. It would show that you, as an employer, had taken steps to ensure that the new employee was properly instructed in all health and safety aspects related to his induction. You may need to make special provision for someone who has a disability.

Firms that make or market a range of products often have a display of these goods that is used for exhibitions or in the front entrance hall. Part of the induction process could be a talk about these goods and services, illustrated by the exhibits.

For many years a major international distribution company has provided a dedicated service to a well-known high street chain of stores. The service includes collections from manufacturers of food and textiles, and includes daily delivery to stores. Adherence to strict time schedules and a high level of accuracy in quantities delivered is vital. To achieve the high standard of efficiency required, it was laid down from the beginning that directors, managers, supervisors, drivers and other key staff would make detailed induction training visits to factories and stores as a fundamental part of their duties.

From the earliest days the distribution company adopted a policy of equal opportunities for women and regularly recruited male and female graduates as management trainees. As the company developed there was a steady increase in the number of women appointed to managerial and supervisory positions in the depots and at head office. This was a positive gain in the relationship with the store chain as many of their managers and supervisors were women. There was a ready acceptance of the women distribution managers by the customer despite the fact that in the road transport industry generally there were few women managers. The company has been less successful in recruiting women as heavy goods vehicle drivers.

The distribution company is convinced that its training programmes helped to accelerate the acceptance of women into managerial positions. Its policy of recruiting able men and women graduates has been a major factor in maintaining a high standard of service and a sound working relationship with its retail customer over a period of 30 years.

Personal development plan

The final item on the checklist refers to a personal development programme. The extent to which this is formalized and the amount of detail will depend on the kind of work involved. The first part of the programme will be the training needed by the newcomer to enable him to do his first job. A full description of how to design, deliver and evaluate training is covered in numerous textbooks. It is important, in helping people to learn in a diverse workforce, to recognize some key facts:

- never generalize about an individual's ability to learn on the basis of irrelevant facts such as age, gender or disability;

- the best way to train an individual depends on the attitudes, knowledge, skill and understanding to be imparted, and on the person's preferred learning styles;

● many people can learn a great deal if the lessons are broken down into small portions, and often retain that learning very effectively;

● it is wrong to assume that older people are less capable than young people at acquiring new skills and knowledge: for the most part it simply is not true;

● for people to learn effectively they must be motivated both by the learning process and by the use to be made of the learning;

● adults generally learn best by being shown how to do things correctly and having this reinforced through practice and sympathetic feedback. Presenting a number of ways a task should not be done is rarely as effective;

● an individual's learning is often influenced by cultural background and previous experience. Many people use analogies with previous experiences to solve problems quickly and to learn by building on their existing knowledge and skills;

● one way to help people to be flexible in their work is to structure their learning with a lot of opportunities to 'discover' knowledge and the way to undertake tasks.

Use the above checklist to ensure that the people who do the training have taken on board the key lessons of diversity. In dealing with a group of people of mixed ethnic backgrounds, mixed gender, age and disability you will find that patience will be required and people will not learn at the same rate or in the same way. It is, of course, essential to ensure that no risk to health or safety is involved when selecting training methods.

> ▶ Ensure that the people who do the training have taken on board the key lessons of diversity

Once the initial training has been accomplished, the individual may be encouraged to develop further skills and to improve the skills acquired. Regular reviews of performance are essential, both to ensure continued progress and to reassure and to motivate the individual. This is particularly important if the person is at a disadvantage for any reason. The research on equality confirms the importance of maintaining the individual's self-respect and motivation to succeed. The organization's supportive culture is essential for this to work, and at the individual's level, for her manager and her workplace colleagues to personify this.

Above all, ensure that people are rewarded for their learning achievements by seeing the results of their work and being given generous praise and encouragement when it is due.

Progress review

A month or two after the newcomer has been inducted it is worthwhile to review the individual's progress and to ensure that he is happy in his work, encountering no problems and doing a satisfactory job of work. This can be built into the performance reviews referred to above or it can be a separate exercise, perhaps carried out by the human resources department.

Progress checklist

? Are you confident that you have an effective induction process, suitable for any individual drawn from a diverse labour force?

? Does your organization have a carefully prepared general induction checklist?

? Do you have a method for adapting this checklist to the needs of each newcomer?

? Have you got a system that ensures that a named individual is in charge of the overall induction process for each newcomer?

? Have you checked to see that health and safety matters are taken fully into account at every stage?

? Does your checklist include a personal development plan or a training programme for every newcomer?

? Are your training methods fully in tune with a workforce of diverse people?

? For each newcomer, have you assigned responsibility for a review of progress?

? Is every manager committed to your induction policy and procedures?

? Do all the members of your workforce understand the company's policy on diversity and how it applies to the induction process? Are they committed to this policy?

9

Developing people

In the previous chapter we drew attention to the importance of initial training and its relation to the induction process. Employees need to learn how to do their jobs. But jobs change and new skills and knowledge must be acquired. Some employees will want to progress beyond the responsibilities they have when they start working for you.

Development review

Many organizations have a procedure whereby each employee is interviewed at least once a year to determine how their work is progressing and what they need to do to develop their full potential and to maximize their contribution to the success of the enterprise. The extent to which this process is formalized and recorded varies from organization to organization, and also depends on the nature of the work involved. Experience has shown that some form of recording is an essential component of an effective employee development system.

For a variety of reasons some people in your organization may feel that they are not gaining the recognition they deserve for their work or the development of their potential. Even when skills and knowledge have been developed some people feel that they do not get the promotion they deserve. These may well be some of the key points that arise from your initial fact-finding activity (Chapter 3).

The line manager concerned generally carries out these performance and development reviews, often with support from the human resource specialists. It is vital that managers are properly trained for this difficult task. Without training, managers are likely to focus narrowly on the department's task in hand, and to see the individual's development only in the context of the section. Managers may need particular help in assessing the learning and development needs of people who come from a different cultural background, or who speak a different first language. Managers may also need help in conversing with someone who has hearing difficulties.

The manager's manager often oversees this process. There are two advantages to this procedure. The more senior person will be able to take the broader view of the individual's development, and she should also ensure fairness and consistency in the judgements made by different managers who report to her.

A number of measures have been used with success in helping people in particular groups to develop their potential and to gain recognition for their work, for example with women workers, black people and people who have specific disabilities. It is a sad fact that we all tend to underestimate the abilities and potential of people with whom we find it difficult to communicate, and people who have a disability.

How people learn

In order to perform a job well individuals require appropriate attitudes, knowledge, skill and understanding. A full discussion of this complex subject is outside the scope of this book, but there are some important factors to be borne in mind. People learn when they react to the phenomena that they sense, see, feel, taste or smell. If there is no reaction, there is no learning, however expertly information is presented. People learn in different ways, and they learn a good deal from observing other people. Many will be quick to discern discrepancies between the way people are supposed to behave (for example to conform to the organization's diversity policies) and the way they actually behave.

There are many ways that people acquire knowledge (reading, listening to people and recorded material, observing) and it is important to choose appropriate methods. Remember that knowledge can be lost, especially if it is not used and constantly reviewed. Understanding and skills take longer to acquire, but tend to stay with you longer.

Attitudes are built up over time, and are influenced by external pressures (peer groups, authority figures, respected people, the media) as much as by rational arguments. If you want to change attitudes, then you need to combine explanation and discussion methods with a set of rules that people are expected to obey. When the rational argument, the people pressure and the 'rules' are aligned, attitudes generally change in all but the most individually minded people.

▶ **People learn by having an experience to which they react**

In essence people learn by having an experience to which they react, and this needs to be reinforced (a) by a review and often (b) by trials with feedback and guidance, particularly when developing skills. The secret of success is, therefore, to create the right learning experiences and opportunities for reflection, trials and feedback. In constructing these experiences one will need to take account of any gender or cultural differences that could influence the individual's reaction.

A large hospital trust (Guy's and St Thomas' Hospital Trust, London) found that although it employed a large number of black women, few had reached management positions. Catherine Roberts, a consultant, was brought in and organized a special development programme for black women as a series of three-day events over a period of months.

Fourteen participants started the programme, coming from several professional disciplines including audit, nursing, midwifery, therapies and management. Their ages ranged from mid-20s to early 50s. Ground rules for the programme included the agreement for participants to challenge any racist or discriminatory comments and assumptions, to speak as little or as much as they wished, and to reinforce positive feedback. They were under no obligation to tell anyone else about the programme or its content. In an introductory exercise people shared common ground and explored their differences. Participants became involved in the design of the programme as they identified individual learning objectives and agreed the content to be covered. Themes included self-presentation, confidence, applying for promotion and increasing personal impact.

The group invited speakers, including role models, mentors from the trust and coaching experts. Some members of the group shadowed senior people to see what their jobs involved. The chair and the chief executive of the trust visited the group. As part of its work the group prepared a series of recommendations to the chief executive. The group continued to meet on a monthly basis. Within 18 months, two members of the group had been promoted. A course for black men has been conducted and a further course is planned to sustain the effort to reduce barriers. (Catherine Roberts can be contacted at RobertsCE@aol.com)

Perhaps the most significant fact is the crucial importance of motivation in the learning process. People learn so much more quickly and effectively when they really want to acquire the knowledge and skills. You must not assume that what will motivate a prime-age Caucasian male will have the same impact on a woman, or an Asian, or an older worker. In particular, people from other cultures may well have different values that need to be taken into account. This is covered more fully in Chapter 13. In addition to the motivation that arises from the outcome of a learning programme, the process itself should have rewards built into it to motivate the learner. Most people will be motivated to learn by some of the following factors, that is when the individual:

- can complete a task well and recognize that this has occurred;
- receives praise for a job well done;
- appreciates belonging to a successful team;
- sees how his work fits into the overall picture;
- considers himself informed – about the organization and the future;
- believes he is being rewarded fairly and that his work is valued.

What people perceive and feel about the situation is more important than what you see as reality. You may consider that they are treated fairly, but if they do not see it that way, it is their perception that will influence their motivation – and their behaviour.

It is important to remember that there are cultures in which the ability to contribute to the wellbeing of the group to which you belong is more important – and a greater motivation – than achieving personal goals. This cuts across some of the management theories that are derived from studies in western cultures.

Learning on the job

Where routine activities are carried out it is often possible to construct a checklist of procedures and to establish straightforward training programmes to enable people to learn how to follow these procedures. These checklists and procedures may need to be modified if one of your workers is disabled, as you may need to introduce different equipment (*see* Chapter 14). If skills are learned on the job, the person giving the instruction and supervising the learner must be properly trained (*see* Chapter 15).

▶ **What people perceive and feel about the situation is most important**

When individuals are required to make decisions, some form of coaching is required where the manager or an experienced worker can talk through these decisions with the learner. When the individual needs to acquire a substantial body of knowledge and understanding, some off-the-job activity may be required.

Learning off the job

Off-the-job courses and workshops may pose particular problems for disabled people unless proper consideration is given to their needs beforehand. The provisions you have made within your organization to help people with hearing, seeing or mobility difficulties may not be reflected in the training venue. Particular regard must be paid to safety considerations.

Your preparation must also take into account any gender, language or cultural problems that might arise. In some cultures it is not usual for women to stay away from home, for example, and this must be considered if you are arranging residential accommodation. Some people may have special food and drink requirements, for cultural or health reasons. People who care for children or for elderly or infirm relatives may need to make special arrangements – and this may cost money.

Preparing for promotion

The selection process for recruitment or promotion is covered in Chapter 5. Here we are concerned with the help some people may need in preparing themselves for promotion, both in terms of building up a track record and in preparing for the process itself. Some people may not wish to seek, or may not be equipped to seek, a higher position. In such cases there may still be room for improvement and development within the job, without pressure to strive for promotion.

Building up a track record is something that some people seem to do effortlessly. They complete tasks, produce results and reports that get noticed by the people above them. But in some cultures this may not be the way to behave. Someone who is self-effacing may just not get noticed, so when people are considering the individual for promotion this person does not come to mind. What is worse, such individuals may not apply because they are not conscious of the value of their work.

> ▶ Some people don't apply for promotion because they are not conscious of their own worth

In counselling women at work, we have found many who do not realize that you get promoted because you convince senior managers that you will be able to do the next job up the ladder – not the one you are doing today. Such people need to be advised that they should talk to their boss and seek opportunities to demonstrate some of the abilities relevant to the more senior job – and to see that this is noted, not just by the boss at the time but in the annual appraisal interview record as well.

People need to be clear about the basis on which promotion is granted so that they may be able to work methodically towards achieving this goal. People who come from the same culture and background seem to belong to in-groups that discuss such matters, albeit informally, and in this way they get a sense of what is required without being formally told. But people in a minority who belong to a different culture may not be a part of this in-group and the conversations that take place. They do not pick up these vibes about what is expected. One approach that has helped to overcome this cultural divide is mentoring (see below).

If the selection process is to include preliminary tests such as written examinations or assessment centres, for example, some of your people may be able to cope better with these than others. You must ensure that the test does not discriminate in any irrelevant manner. The ability to cope with such tests may not be a good predictor of how well they would perform the job.

People should be able to sit the same kind of tests beforehand in a non-threatening environment, just to get the feel of the situation. They should be given feedback, not only on their performance but also in terms of how they prepared themselves for the ordeal and how this could be improved. People who learn less quickly than others may still perform jobs well – sometimes better than the person who appears to learn quickly but fails to grasp the subject thoroughly. People with any communication difficulty (language, sight, hearing, literacy) must be given time and help to understand and absorb ideas and procedures.

▶ **Coping with a test may not predict how well a person will perform the job**

Mentoring support

People often need support that is not specifically related to job skills but rather to the way they approach the job and relate to others. A mentor can often help. The word mentor has a number of interpretations and here we are concerned with a more senior person who is not in the chain of command. This individual can meet with the individual, chat about the job, the person's progress, plans for learning and development. The mentor can talk through problems and offer some coaching, for example on how to approach senior people or colleagues in other departments, or how to tackle learning problems. The mentor may act as a counsellor, helping the individual to make important decisions by acting as a sounding board.

The mentor may open doors, enabling the individual to meet people who can help with advice and perhaps instruction in specific skills. Research on open learning has emphasized the key importance of the non-technical mentor who can help people to plan how they will learn and how they will organize their lives to achieve learning goals.

Such support is distinct from the help and support that the line manager can and should give to individuals to aid their development. The line manager tends to focus, quite rightly, on getting the job done, but in many organizations the development of staff is a clear responsibility of the line manager.

An organization with a substantial number of black employees found that relatively few black people gained promotion to middle management position, yet they seemed to be on average no less capable than their white colleagues. The organization instituted a system whereby a number of senior white people were asked to act as mentors to promising black employees. Over a period of time, as these mentors and black employees started to communicate and the black employees started to recognize that the way was open and to learn how to prepare for progression, the number of black promotions increased. There were also other factors that helped, for example concerned with the selection process.

Progress checklist

[?] Do you have a system that enables each person to review his development and to plan to improve?

[?] Do the methods used for helping people to learn recognize the different approaches, selected according to the nature of the learning required?

[?] Do your procedures take full account of the differences in strategies that people use to learn?

[?] Does your organization reward people for the learning they achieve and provide motivation for learning within the learning process?

[?] Are on-the-job learning activities well organized, with competent instructors and well-documented procedures?

[?] Where off-the-job learning is required, do your arrangements take account of the needs of people, for example from a different culture, or who have a disability, or who have commitments as carers at home?

[?] Are you convinced that people of all kinds have appropriate help in preparing themselves for promotion?

[?] Have you considered the role of mentoring in your organization?

10

Teamwork

Teamwork can be a feature of the whole organization, not just confined to small groups of people. An individual team is typically made up of 3–12 people. Two people can work as a team, but as the group gets larger than 12, communication become more difficult – although not impossible – to manage. The psychology, however, changes if the group of people becomes too large.

Success factors

Team effectiveness depends on a number of factors – the ability and personalities of team members, the number of people involved, the nature of the task, and the team members' commitment to it. There is plenty of hard evidence to show that the most effective teams are made up of people with diverse personalities. A group of people with very similar personalities will find it hard to become an effective team. But forming groups of people with different backgrounds does not guarantee effective teamwork. The urgency of the task, the length of time the team stays together, the organizational roles of the team members and the qualities of the team members all play a part.

There are many examples of groups of people with very different backgrounds forming effective teams – people from different countries, different races, different ages, different genders, different cultures and different languages. To some extent there may also be a culture that is associated with the functions that people perform. There is often a culture difference between scientists and accountants, or between engineers and production people. These cultures manifest themselves in priorities and in language. In considering multinational groups, the culture difference between functions can be as serious a problem as national differences (*see* Chapter 13).

> ▶ Forming a group with people of different backgrounds does not guarantee teamwork

Once you have your mixed group, you will still need to create the conditions conducive to teamwork. The major problem to be overcome in mixed groups is communications (see below). Teamwork depends on four vital factors for success. The group of people who are to function as a team must:

- be committed to a common goal
- respect one another
- know how to work together.

Furthermore, within organizations:

- the climate and managerial style must be conducive to teamwork, if the team's efforts are to contribute effectively to the organization's success.

If you decide to appoint a formal team leader, for example to run a project, the qualities of the individual will be of particular importance. The ability to appreciate the potential worth of every individual irrespective of race, gender, disability, age and so forth will be crucial in a diverse workforce. Many teams require someone to act as the leader because of the organizational context. In a mature team different people may act as leaders at different times according to the task.

By taking into account the roles that team members assume, there are ways in which you can enhance team effectiveness. Furthermore, by paying attention to the components of the job, the work roles, and the functional roles of the people concerned, it is possible for people to learn to achieve their joint and individual tasks more efficiently.

Dr Meredith Belbin's research (Belbin, 1999) uses a colour-coding system to identify different categories of work activity (for example blue work where there is adherence to prescribed methods, and white work where there is considerable discretion and personal initiative). Once these ideas have been mastered people have a way of communicating about jobs that transcends language barriers. Using these methods, a mature team can learn to manage both the team roles and the work roles, distributing work between its members for maximum effect. Dr Belbin has also pointed out (Belbin, 2000) the importance of size in the way that a number of people can work together.

A small number of people can work effectively as a team if the conditions are right. But if the number of people is increased, a point is reached where the interaction between them is such that they can no longer be described as a team. The psychology of the way team members interact and the benefits that flow from this are distinct from that of the way people interact in large groups. People in small teams also stand a better chance of getting to know each other, their strengths and weaknesses, and the potential contribution that each can make to the team's success. Such knowledge and understanding is even more critical in multicultural groups.

> ▶ People in small teams stand a better chance of getting to know each other

Team goals

Many organizations fail to capitalize on teamwork because they do not take the trouble to ensure that each group of people has a clear understanding of how they fit into the operation, how they relate to the work of other groups and what they need to do to help other groups to succeed. The group's goals must be clearly defined, yet not so tightly that there is no room for improvement on the basis of understanding the needs of others within the organization. Goals should also leave room for alternative means of achievement. This level of understanding is essential if people are to be wholeheartedly committed to the group's goal and the organization's overall objectives. To motivate team members, the team's shared goals must be achievable with effort.

The group will become a team only if the members embrace the common goal and know how to work together to achieve it. Helping a team to understand and embrace common goals may need patience if the members are drawn from a variety of cultures. People from some cultures are content with fairly narrowly defined parameters, but others want to know a lot more of the background and context before embracing particular ideas or goals.

▶ **Many organizations fail to capitalize on teamwork**

Motivational drives vary from person to person in different cultures and in people at different ages and stages of their careers. Some people will readily work with others of different cultural backgrounds. But in some cultures there will be a reluctance to share goals or to work closely with people of a different gender or faith, or with people of a different generation.

Many organizations want people to work in teams where hierarchy is almost forgotten, but in some cultures class and the hierarchical position are highly valued and jealously guarded. In such cases senior managers will need patiently to create an open culture within the organization, a culture that will enable senior people to work alongside junior staff in a team with a common endeavour.

Team workers

Becoming a team player means sharing the goals of the team, recognizing and welcoming the contribution of other team members, playing a full part in achieving team success and accepting responsibility with others. If you enable people to develop the skills of team working, teams will form spontaneously when a few people recognize that they need to work together to solve a problem or to meet a challenge.

The skills of a team worker can be summarized as follows (Johnson, 1995):

- identify shared goals
- support colleagues
- listen
- contribute constructively
- review experiences and learn from them.

Apart from the communication problem, the most difficult attribute to encourage in a diverse group is respect for every individual. There is a danger that any individual in a minority will find it difficult to earn respect. This is made harder if there is some obvious distinction such as age, gender, colour or an evident disability. The single woman in an otherwise male team, the black person in an otherwise white team, the old chap in an otherwise young team, the blind member of an otherwise sighted team – each has been seen as the odd one out.

> ▶ **An individual in a minority may find it difficult to earn respect.**

There is no simple answer to this problem. Progress can be made when you build a culture of respect for every individual, incorporating this into the company policy, the employment terms and conditions, and the management style. Many companies have explicitly included respect for every individual as a cornerstone of their people management policies.

Part of the consideration that team members will have for each other will involve taking into account any difficulty that an individual might face. For example, if a team member has hearing difficulties, or mobility problems, this will be taken into account in the physical location chosen for team meetings. If a member has a language problem, the team will consider cost-effective ways of dealing with this.

Some years ago it was difficult to arrange for interpreters to be present at every gathering of small groups of experts and officials in the European Commission. A solution that was sometimes satisfactory was to hold the meeting in two languages. The people who attended these meetings could often speak French and understand English, or speak English and understand French. Most people find it easier to speak a language they are familiar with, and to listen to another language that they do not speak so well. At one meeting where the Dutch, the German and the Irish spoke English, and the French, the Belgian and the Italian spoke French, the business was concluded successfully.

Communications

If you want to understand what an individual is saying, you must recognize that his words mean what he says they mean – not what you think they mean. Words are not precise units of communication. They often have emotional and subtle overtones that imbue them with a particular import. When words are translated there are often shades of meaning. To ignore these vital factors is to court disaster in communications. Often in the hurly-burly of energetic teamwork there is no time for lengthy explanations and people resort to jargon words, acronyms or abbreviations that are specific to the profession or the task in hand. A newcomer to the team may find this use of language difficult to grasp at the outset, particularly if he or she comes from a different culture or has a different first language.

Some people take longer to think about problems and to formulate their thoughts to contribute to discussions. This is particularly acute if there are problems of language or unfamiliar technical terms involved.

There is no short-cut solution. Each team member must be encouraged to ask questions whenever she is unable to follow the argument or cannot understand the words or phrases being used. Team members, and especially the team leader, must have the patience to listen to such questions and to respond. Team members must learn that this is both faster and more effective teamwork in the long run. Speed at the expense of understanding on the part of team members may be justified in a real emergency – and even then the advantage is often doubtful.

> **Words often have emotional and subtle overtones, and nuances of meaning**

The effectiveness of teams is maximized when every member is enabled to play a full part. Someone who does not understand may well make a mistake later on, when there will not be time to discuss the matter.

Choosing teams

It is tempting to specify precisely the kind of people – in terms of expertise and psychological profiles – that you need to make up your perfect team. In the real world you are often unable even to approach this situation. Teams tend to be chosen because of the particular skill mix required rather than the psychological profiles of the people concerned. For example, for a project team in a wire manufacturing company you may bring together a machine operator, a technician, a fitter and an engineer to solve a manufacturing problem. You will not have the luxury of a range of people to choose from.

A distribution company seeking new business might bring together people with expertise in marketing, logistics, finance, quality management and human resources to prepare and present the tender. Management will usually have limited scope in choosing these people. If you are developing business in another country it makes sense to learn about the country, its rules and regulations, and its culture. It would be even wiser to have a person from that country on the team.

However, insights on personality profiles and team roles can help even if you have limited scope to choose the teams on that basis. Knowing the composition of the team usually gives some clues on ways in which you can help the team to be more effective.

Building teamwork

If you already have effective teamwork and know how to build it, you can skip this section. But if you want to generate more ideas and feedback from people you will need to work harder to create a culture of openness, honesty and trust. Trust takes time to build and is easily lost. Dishonesty and inconsistency will quickly destroy trust. This is why the first work must be at management level. Trust is often more difficult to build between people of different cultures or backgrounds. We may not know how to interpret the non-verbal signals that are such an important part of building relationships.

▶ **People need 'space' to contribute ideas**

People need 'space' to contribute ideas. This space needs to be created by management. It means leaving decisions open, that is having clear goals but with the methods open to suggestions. It means consulting people genuinely – and often – having first determined where they can make a difference. People who are in a minority in an organization tend to find that they have even less 'space' than others in contributing ideas and taking decisions.

Senior managers must be truly supportive, both of teamwork and of the concept of diversity in teamwork. If not, even a casual remark can be enough to reveal lack of real support. Senior managers need to work with middle managers on more precise goals for the medium term – the progress aimed at in, say, six months. These goals should include tangible improvements based on measures of performance that your people consider sensible and reasonable.

Do not fall into the trap of choosing measures of achievement or performance just because they are easy to obtain. The measures you use must be valuable to you and to your people. There should also be goals that are concerned with observable behaviour. The respect referred to above must be translated into actions – acknowledging people, listening to their points of view, including them in the informal information network, recognizing their contribution to the matter in hand.

Managers need to work out what it will be like when people do come up with ideas, and how they will handle this. You may need to bring about a major change in management style and organizational culture, and if so you need to understand and anticipate how this will work. A simple ABC might help you think about this.

Attitudes on the part of management and other workers will need to change. Senior people discussing why the change needs to take place and what it will be like to work in this new environment start this process. Managers may fear loss of authority. They need to be reassured that their authority remains, but will be exercised in new ways. They may fear loss of work, but this loss (as workers take more decisions themselves) should provide time for more valuable activities, such as planning more effectively. Later discussions with your workers will be designed to establish a new working relationship between them and the management team.

You may need to emphasize that these changes are not to save money or staff, but to improve the effectiveness of the department and the organization. The benefit for workers is threefold: (a) it will be a happier place to work as every individual becomes more valued and communications become less constrained, (b) a more successful firm usually means, on balance, a more secure job, (c) people who learn to operate effectively in a team culture actually become more employable if and when they decide to move on.

Behaviour needs to become more spontaneous and constructive. It is helped by a set of informal rules that people can work out for themselves. In a diversified workforce, these must not be imposed from above but evolved as people see that a different set of behaviours is appropriate. This behaviour change must start with the management team who need to set a consistent example. The rules will include ideas such as:

- we will always praise genuinely whenever possible;
- we will always criticize constructively;
- negative criticism will be considered inappropriate behaviour;
- every suggestion will be carefully considered and the results of this consideration fed to the people concerned – promptly;

● we will make every effort to listen carefully to what people are telling us and try to understand, even if at first sight the ideas appear unhelpful.

Managers must be prepared to be seen to change their minds in the light of ideas and suggestions put forward by the workers. No change without appropriate consultation should become the norm. This consultation should include people with expertise, and people who will be affected by the change.

Individual behaviour will be influenced by the way team members are rewarded. If people are rewarded only for individual effort without reference to their team contribution, the reward system will act as a disincentive to teamwork.

Culture may be defined simply as 'the way we do things round here'. The informal rules outlined above will form an essential component of the new culture. Blame will be apportioned only after every other factor has been taken into account. Whenever a mishap occurs this will be thoroughly investigated to establish the causes and people will be blamed only for repeated carelessness or deliberate sabotage. This is sometimes called a 'no-blame' culture. The culture should be outward looking, focused on achieving results together in ways that everyone can share. The emphasis will be on positive, collaborative problem solving. Whatever their background or appearance, team players will be valued. A further cultural norm should be that people are encouraged to raise problems, not hide them. People must never be punished for identifying a difficulty. This should be seen as an opportunity to improve.

In a forward-facing, outward-looking, open and honest culture, it is important to develop people's problem-solving and teamwork skills. Lateral and linear problem-solving procedures and creative methods should be acquired by everybody and used regularly. Above all, emphasize the common cause and the sharing of effort to achieve the goals in ways that will benefit everybody.

Progress checklist

? Have you and your senior colleagues recognized how teamwork can be successfully applied in your organization?

? Does your organization ensure that everyone is clear about the team's goals and how they contribute to organizational success?

[?] Have you created a culture of respect for every team member?

[?] Have you checked that communications are at a high standard both within and across teams?

[?] How do you choose your teams? Have you taken into account the differences between people and how this can be managed?

[?] What measures have you taken to build teams and nurture teamwork throughout the organization?

11

Flexibility in practice

Advantages

Flexibility is one of the major components of a strategy to manage diversity. It provides opportunities for very real business advantages, and it is also a tool in releasing the potential of the workforce. This flexibility may, for example, be concerned with job roles, working time or shift patterns.

From the employer's point of view flexible working practices and flexible working hours can be used to improve the effectiveness of the use of employees' time and expertise. From the employees' viewpoint, it can enable individuals to cope with home and family commitments, or even to indulge in their favourite pastimes. When coal mines were closed it was found that is some areas ex-miners did not readily settle into the normal routine of daytime factory work as this did not allow them to look after their racing pigeons – a pastime suited to the shift patterns in the mines.

Flexible working hours may also be of value to the employer in other ways. For example, some employers whose business is subject to severe seasonal variations employ a number of trained people working part-time.

When the business becomes very busy, these part-time staff can increase the time they spend at work, helping the firm to cope with the workload without the need to employ new people who will need training.

Parents responsible for the care of young children and other carers (people who look after infirm or elderly relatives) find that full-time work to pre-set hours can limit their ability to partic-

> ▶ Flexible working hours can be of value to both employers and employees

ipate in paid employment. In such cases flexible hours of work can open doors for them and also extend the range of skilled people available to employers. Flexibility in terms of the place of work or the tasks to be performed can open the way for carers or for people with disabilities to obtain gainful employment.

At one time caring responsibilities were considered to be a problem that only women faced, but nowadays men often have a major role in fulfilling family responsibilities. This can apply to young men with children or to people at any age with elderly or infirm relatives. Caring responsibilities may be particularly acute for single parents (men or women) and this applies equally to single-sex partners bringing up children as to male-female partnerships.

Workers beyond the normal retiring age may want to continue to work but not to have full-time jobs. Flexibility in working hours and job roles may prove to be the solution. In many countries there are laws controlling the conditions of employment of people who are employed on a part-time or contract basis, and these will need to be checked when establishing a different pattern of working hours or other variations in the contract of employment.

Hours of work

The drive to reduce costs and improve the quality of services by greater efficiency combined with the need to provide services more closely aligned with customer demands has dramatically transformed the hours that people work and the range of tasks that they are required to perform. In some organizations the changes have led to opportunities for more flexibility in the hours worked. For example, the long opening hours of retail stores and the pattern of customer visits demands a complex system of shift patterns for staff. Often this means that on an individual basis it is possible to work around home and family commitments.

In other organizations the demands of the job limit this flexibility. Ambulance crews on emergency call-out duties need to work complete eight-hour shifts to provide an effective service. Even in these circumstances, however, it is possible to vary the shifts that individuals are required to work to help people who find full-time work difficult.

A young woman working full-time as a paramedic for the Two Shires Ambulance NHS Trust wanted to spend more time with her family following the birth of her baby. The trust arranged for her contract to be varied so that she was required to work a minimum number of shifts during the year on a mutually agreed basis. From time to time paramedics fall ill and have to be temporarily replaced. The trust then calls on people such as the young woman to fill the gap. The woman can accept or not, provided she fulfils the number of shifts during the year. Such an arrangement is helpful to the individual, and to the trust, and it is also valuable for paramedics who have other caring responsibilities (e.g. for disabled or elderly relatives) and for whom full-time work is not a viable option.

Over recent years the trust has increased the proportion of women employed and has also witnessed a major shift in culture. Some years ago ambulance paramedic crews were predominantly men, but now about 27 per cent of these front-line staff are women. Women are also increasingly moving into front-line management positions. The next challenge will be to increase the representation of Asian, Chinese and Afro-Caribbean people on the workforce to reflect the population served by the trust.

There are also many jobs that can be shared and this can work to the advantage of both the employer and the employees concerned. Often, however, for job-sharing to work well there must be good working relationships between the people involved.

At one time, Dr Eunice Belbin, the Director of a training research organization, employed two secretaries who each worked two-and-a-half days a week. Jean would work from Monday morning until Wednesday lunchtime, and Lee would take over and work until Friday afternoon. The women worked well together, and the two secretaries would each ensure that (a) they kept each other fully informed on the work in hand, and (b) that the boss was fully supported. Wherever possible, each would seek to complete any complex piece of typing work (for example a research report) before handing over the reins to her colleague.

If one was unwell, the other would be prepared to stand in, and they were prepared to put in extra time to cover for each other for holidays and days off. When there was an 'open day', both would attend to help with the organization and the exhibits. This arrangement worked well for a number of years.

The employment offered by such organizations as nursing or home-care agencies is also flexible, often allowing employees to choose their hours of work very precisely to avoid working, for example, when they have to get children off to school. Provided the agencies have other workers who are prepared to work these hours, the service can be provided. As in the case of job-sharing, people must be prepared to 'give and take' if this is to work effectively. This requires the employer to generate and sustain a supportive culture.

> **Good working relationships are essential for job-sharing to work well**

Location

The dramatic improvement in communication methods means that there are many jobs that can be undertaken at home, and many jobs where a proportion of the work can be done at home. Some people can spend some time at home, some time visiting clients and some time in the office or workshop at the employer's premises. When on the employer's premises, staff can be 'hot-desking', using one of a number of the workplaces on a temporary basis. Each desk or workstation will need to be properly equipped, and people who use a computer terminal will need passwords to gain access to their work and data. Each worker who uses these workstations in this way may also need a secure space, for example a cupboard or a filing cabinet, to store papers etc.

Whenever people work without close supervision the employer can choose to impose a complex system of checks and controls, or to generate a culture of trust and support. In practice there must be a mixture of both trust and sensible controls if success is to be achieved in this type of working relationship. At one extreme raw material can be provided and completed articles collected and paid for on an item-by-item basis, as in the rag trade of old. The quality can be checked and very little trust is required. However, when this type of close control and piecework payment is not possible, the manager needs to build up a relationship of trust and mutual endeavour with staff.

Anyone who has had to manage a field force, for example of salespeople, advisors or maintenance engineers, will know the problem of gaining the full-hearted co-operation of every employee. People who spend so much time with your customers need to be encouraged to work for the benefit of your organization as well as for their customers. The members of the field force need to be fully supported, encouraged and informed.

If you can trust your people and manage the operation, there are distinct advantages in enabling some people to spend some time working at home. In many 'considerative' tasks people find they

▶ **A lot of work can be done at home – in some sectors**

can get more done per hour at home. It can be difficult to be creative in a busy office. (Of course, it can be equally difficult to work to the sound of bawling children!) If you have fewer people using workstations at work, you need less equipment and less office space. When your location is in the centre of a city, this may be a powerful consideration. Such arrangements are particularly suitable for people with mobility problems, or people who care for young children or elderly or infirm relatives.

In managing professional people off-site, managers will need to learn how to set tasks by output – in other words, they will need to specify what they expect people to produce. In the past managers have tended to manage by telling people what to do, not what to produce.

Job roles

For many years organizations have been multiskilling, that is, they have been training people to do a wider range of tasks. The classic case is the training of fitters to undertake some of the tasks normally undertaken by electrical craftsmen, and vice versa. Once the training has been completed so that the craftspeople can do a range of tasks, their job roles become more flexible. In more recent years these skills have been extended to include electronic skills as so much equipment has electronic components. Much of the maintenance work has been simplified by integrated circuits and the like.

The examples of multiskilling are legion. Warehouse operatives are now trained in computer skills so that they can use the terminals to keep track of stock movements and requirements. Executives learn to type so that they can enter their data and write correspondence directly into their computers and send e-mails.

In a truly empowered workforce, an individual would tackle any task that needed to be done if he had the ability to do the job. You will not hear people saying that a task 'is not my job'. Few organizations are likely to approach such a state, but the principles involved can be used to enhance flexibility. Some companies have abandoned the restrictive concept of job descriptions and now define the roles of their employees in imaginative and flexible ways that enable their people to develop their jobs and roles over time, and to make full use of the opportunities to improve the effectiveness of the organization, their personal development and working conditions.

> **Some companies have abandoned the restrictive concept of job descriptions**

At Honda (UK) employees meet formally with their bosses twice a year to agree on objectives for the following year. Some of these objectives are specific to the individual and will normally be concerned with personal development or achievement aims within the work context. One individual chose as one of his personal objectives to work with a charity related to the motor trade and this was agreed. Remaining objectives will be specific to the work tasks and some are shared with other members of the team. These procedures are underpinned by the Honda policy of respect for the individual. The 'personal review process' is designed to assist in the performance of a job to the best of an individual's ability while maximizing job satisfaction and contribution to the overall business, and also to identify individual and company training requirements, highlighting individual potential and career development.

The flexibility that enables individuals to fashion their own jobs within the context of achieving the organization's goals aids in the release of human potential in the workplace. This approach is particularly positive for people who have some form of disadvantage. If managers are properly trained to be sensitive to the needs and potential of every individual, they will help people with a disability or a problem associated with language, religion or family commitments.

Work organization

There are many ways of organizing people to achieve results and many ways to examine how an organization operates. In many modern organizations the number of layers of management has been reduced. People are becoming more involved in the decisions made in the workplace. Often individuals have more responsibility for making decisions and producing results. To make decisions people need information, training and authority.

A vast amount of relevant information is now available adjacent to the machines in production departments, at the warehouse terminal and on the salesperson's laptop. People can base their decisions on real-time data. But managers need to be sure that people are making the best decisions in the interest of the organization. For this, two more conditions must be fulfilled. Decision makers must be trained to understand the logic of decision making and the impact of different decisions on the effectiveness of the organization, and they must be committed to the organization's goals.

> ▶ **People are becoming more involved in the decisions made in the workplace**

The level of co-operation required cannot be achieved unless the organization has developed a culture that respects people in all their diversity and the contribution that they can make. Opening up the organization in this way may expose the decision-making process to alternative ways of thinking if there are material cultural differences in the make-up of the workforce.

The downside is that this may slow up decision making as people view problems from different angles. The upside is that the quality of decision making will almost certainly improve. Managers sometimes pay a lot of money to attend courses to learn about alternative ways of looking at problems. You may have people with these qualities on your staff! But you may need to take time to enable people to recognize the distinctive contribution that different ways of thinking can add to the quality of decisions. One of the key advantages of teamwork is the way that people who look at problems from different viewpoints can work together to obtain better, sometimes more imaginative, solutions.

The manager from the Japanese company wanted a licence to fish for tuna in the ocean around the Solomon Islands. The 'man from the ministry' in the capital, Honoraria, granted the licence to enhance the prosperity of the islands. But the islanders found that the fishing fleet was depleting the stocks of tuna fish on the in-shore fishing grounds where the local inhabitants fished with poles. Their tribal chiefs made representations to the minister and other politicians. The problem was recognized and the licence with the Japanese company was renegotiated to reduce the impact on the in-shore fish stocks. The licence also required the Japanese company to buy surplus fish caught by the islanders. The optimum solution was found only when all points of view had been taken into account.

Flexible options

The pattern of trade now offers enormous scope for ingenuity in the way people are employed, both with regard to hours of work, shift patterns, location and job roles. Within this framework employers can offer opportunities that enable carers and people with disabilities to achieve gainful employment and to make their full contribution to society.

Opening up organizations to people's ideas and providing opportunities for more involvement in decisions can improve the quality of decisions and the effectiveness of the operation. This is particularly true if the workforce is diverse, provided a culture of respect and involvement is encouraged.

Progress checklist

? Have you carefully considered ways in which flexibility can improve your operation?

? Do the working hours in different parts of your organization enable you to employ a more diverse workforce?

? Have you considered the extent to which people working off-site (for example at home) could bring real benefits to your organization, and also offer employment opportunities to people who would find regular attendance at your premises for the normal working day a problem?

? Are you confident that you have fully taken into account the impact of new technology on the roles of your employees and the tasks they have to perform?

[?] Are you reaping the full benefits of a workforce where more people are involved in decision making?

[?] Have you opened up people's perception to the richness of diversity in meeting challenges and solving problems?

12

People-friendly policies

▶ Extend the concept of family friendly

▶ Consider leave for parents and carers

▶ Review childcare provisions

▶ Consider help for other carers

▶ Allow for people's problems with off-site events

▶ Review pensions and medical care provisions

The work-life balance

Many organizations have introduced family-friendly policies. In the main these are concerned with time off to look after children and in some cases the provision of childcare facilities at the workplace or payments to enable parents to purchase childcare to allow them to attend the workplace.

> ▶ Think more widely than in terms of just the traditional family

We consider it important to think more widely than in terms of just the traditional family, although this will probably be a major area for action. Issues such as paternity leave, maternity leave, provision for those who care for relatives, equal treatment of benefits for partners may form an essential part of diversity management activities. In today's society, eldercare must be considered as well as childcare. The provision of spouse pensions is a related issue.

The subject can now be widened to embrace the whole problem of fitting the working life pattern into the way people want to live their lives. For most people part of this balance will involve spending time with the family and following personal interests. For those who have the responsibility of caring for a relative, achieving this balance becomes both more pressing and more difficult.

In the following paragraphs we have often depicted the problem from the carer's viewpoint so that as an employer you can understand the situation and, hopefully, respond in helpful ways, enabling people with family responsibilities to gain employment and contribute to your business. We are aware that in many stressful jobs women, in particular, find it difficult to balance the demands of the job, the home and the family. If these people are making a valuable contribution to the firm it makes sense to provide support. We came across one woman in a high-profile financial post who employed four people to look after her six children while she pursued her career.

▶ **Employees may be caring for relatives who are elderly, infirm or mentally ill**

Although most carers are between 45 and 64, it is a mistake to characterize carers as middle-aged. Some are young children, looking after a parent, and many are past the normal retirement age – also looking after a parent or an elderly aunt or uncle. Some young people have to care for a disabled spouse as well as looking after their children. The need to provide care for a relative can come at any age and any stage. You may find that some of your employees have had to assume this type of responsibility.

We tend to think of caring in relation to disability or physical illness, but in some cases there is a need to care for someone with a mental illness. In many countries there has been (and in some there still is) a stigma attached to mental illness. However, about one in ten of the population will suffer some form of mental illness at some time in their lives. Furthermore, some mild form of mental illness often accompanies physical illness or disability.

Leave

In many countries there are legal provisions that require employers to grant paid or unpaid leave to the parents of young children. In the past this leave has been granted only to mothers, but in today's society where fathers play an increasing role in child rearing, this leave is often granted to them as well. You will need to ensure that your terms and conditions of service comply with the laws that apply to your employees in this respect. If you are embracing comprehensive diversity policies you will need to consider your attitude to families other than the traditional biological-mother-and-father-of-the-children pattern. Frequent divorces, remarriage, and partner changes mean that often the mother is living with a partner who is not the biological father of her children.

Furthermore, adoption rules are changing and children may be living with two people of the same sex in a stable relationship, effectively acting as parents. Your terms and conditions of service may need to reflect this situation in respect of the leave provisions granted to employees who adopt a child.

You may also wish to consider your policy on bereavement leave. Is it still based on the model of a family consisting of heterosexual married partners with two children?

Carers may also need respite leave and for your employees this will normally form part of their normal leave entitlement. However, fixing the dates of their holidays may depend to some extent on their ability to arrange for care for their relative.

Some organizations now grant leave to women undergoing fertility treatment.

Childcare

Parents with young children who want to continue to work must make provision for the care of their children while they attend the workplace. In a two-parent family, one parent may decide to stay at home at crucial periods of time, for example getting the children ready for school and collecting them when the school day ends. This individual may be unemployed, employed on a part-time basis, or self-employed, fitting work around the needs of the children.

Many people who want to stay in touch with working life at this stage may opt for a period of part-time employment with the organization where they previously worked on a full-time basis. Many employers prefer this arrangement as it enables them to make use of the services of people they have trained, with the prospect of them returning to full-time employment at a later stage. In this case the employer will often make arrangements to maintain the skills of the individual concerned. Where this is not the preferred option, for whatever reason, the individual may consider alternative employment that offers the possibility of part-time work or flexible working hours.

The problem for one-parent families is more acute. Here the parent may decide that full-time work is essential to provide a decent income. Thus there will be a number of people who want to work full-time, but who have children who need to be cared for during at least part of the working day. If there are no family members who can assume this role, the alternatives are to use childcare facilities at the workplace (if they exist) or for the parent to pay for childcare at a nursery or play school.

For the employer, this means considering whether or not to provide on-site childcare facilities or the provision of extra cash to enable parents to pay for childcare. This policy needs to be carefully considered in the light of the above paragraphs. Will this apply to stable male/female partners and single-sex partners as well as to married couples and single parents? How will the organization define stable relationships?

Carers National Association is a leading UK organization working to raise awareness with government and society of the needs of carers, including working carers. One of CNA's project officers is herself a carer and benefits from the organization's recognition of and support for the particular needs of employees who juggle work and care. CNA offers a 'mix and match' of practices that she uses when necessary, including:

- flexible working hours – her son attends a residential special school, and on Fridays she starts work early so that she can leave early to pick him up for the weekend;

- home working – she can arrange to work some days from home during school holidays in order to take and pick up her son from activities;

- carers' leave – she uses this in emergencies, anything from her son falling ill to an urgent meeting at the school;

- use of a telephone to speak to her son at the end of his school day.

Most importantly, she knows that her line manager will respond sensitively and *swiftly* when she needs flexibility. Without this, she feels that she would not be able to work effectively; with it, she believes she gives the organization her 100 per cent commitment, balancing work and care without compromising either, a belief which is endorsed by her colleagues. (The e-mail address of CNA is info@ukcarers.org)

Some organizations have a clear policy of providing career breaks for staff who want to stay at home and look after children for an extended period – of years rather than weeks. Experience has shown that if the people on leave are to have a reasonable prospect of returning to a similar job to the one they left, some form of ongoing contact is essential. The contact may take the form of periods of full-time or part-time work or participation in updating courses. The world of work is changing at such a rate that without such provision, people on extended leave find it difficult to resume their former jobs effectively.

Other carers

Much of what has been said about the need to help people who care for children can be applied to people who look after an elderly or infirm relative. Here the problem is not associated with getting children ready for

> ▶ Carers may need to be directed towards help

school, but it may well involve helping someone to get out of bed, use the toilet, have breakfast and help with washing. It may involve taking that individual to a day-care centre or to a hospital appointment. It may involve collecting that individual at a particular time from the day-care centre or hospital.

In many cases there are no suitable day-care facilities and so the elderly relative will need to be set up for the day, perhaps with prepared food, and with a telephone or emergency button provided. In such cases the carer will be contacted if an emergency arises and must be able to respond. In most cases this is likely to arise only on very rare occasions. Unfortunately there are some illnesses where contact is sought so frequently that normal employment for the carer is virtually impossible.

In Chapter 11 we referred to flexible working hours as one way of helping such carers. Help with paying for care is another option, but few employers will be able to afford this unless there is also state aid. A few employers have established day-care centres for the elderly so that their employees can bring these people with them to the workplace.

Many carers find their responsibilities both tiring and stressful, and they are often unaware of the help available. You may be able to help your employees in this position by ensuring that they are fully aware of the support they can receive from public bodies, voluntary organizations and from your own human resources department.

Centrica plc has developed a policy for carers – employees who have long-term or permanent caring responsibilities for seriously sick, elderly or disabled relatives, partners and family. The company is sympathetic to the demands that such responsibilities make on an employee and recognizes that from time to time this can make it difficult for an individual to combine paid work with caring.

The aim of the policy is to ensure that the Centrica Group can recruit and retain employees who have assumed caring responsibilities. Local managers have final discretion concerning leave and other matters covered by the policy, but they are expected to give sympathetic consideration to employees' requests for support. The intention is that this support is based on a shared understanding of the difficulties the employee is facing.

The Centrica carers' policy seeks to ensure that employees are actively encouraged to inform their manager if they are caring for someone, and that this information will be dealt with in a confidential manner. Staff must not be discriminated against on the grounds of their caring responsibilities and the policy also seeks to promote consistency of treatment, taking into account each person's circumstances.

The policy deals with the four key areas of support that carers need: (a) leave, (b) access to a telephone, (c) working arrangements, including the possibility of career breaks and home working, and (d) access to counselling. For each of these areas of concern, sensible and reasonable guidelines and arrangements are outlined. Within these guidelines, arrangements for each employee concerned can be made in the light of the circumstances in the workplace and at home.

Communications

One of the concerns of people who are cared for is their ability to summon help in an emergency. Many older people will want to contact their caring relative rather than 'a stranger' from the ambulance service or a care agency. In the UK, most people in this situation can have an emergency alarm button fitted in their homes so that they can alert the call centre when an emergency occurs. If the emergency is a minor one (that is not requiring the emergency services) it is normal practice to contact the relative. If the emergency services need to be called (for example because of a serious fall or a fire), they would normally want to contact the relative as well as they will have a key to allow access without resort to the stressful step of demolishing the front door.

It is therefore important to consider how the relative can be reached by telephone to enable him to respond, and as an employer you must be sympathetic to the action that needs to be taken. With most carers, this would be a rare event.

Off-site events

The most common occasion when an employee is asked to attend an off-site event is a training course or conference. It is important to take into account people's family commitments and cultural lifestyles in choosing both the time and the place for these events. Avoid religious holidays and events that parents are expected to attend (such as school open days). If the event requires the employee to stay overnight, ensure that the family needs are taken into account and provide help where possible.

You may be able to choose a site where childcare facilities are available, or to help a carer arrange alternative accommodation for the elderly relative. You must determine the extent to which you intend to make such provisions, and you need to establish a policy so that everyone is clear about the help likely to be available.

Pensions and medical care

Many organizations have pension schemes for their employees that include a provision for the spouse (and sometimes the children) of a married person on the death of the employee. You may wish to consider to what extent this provision will apply to partners in stable relationships, whether these are male/female or single-gender partnerships.

Some organizations fund private medical care schemes for their employees and may extend this to include the spouse and children. Again you will need to consider who is included in these schemes.

Progress checklist

? Do your family-friendly policies extend to non-traditional families?

? What provisions do you make for paid or unpaid leave for parents and other carers?

[?] Do you have clear-cut policies to help employees who care for young children?

[?] What help does your organization provide for other carers?

[?] Does your organization have a policy to minimize problems for employees when arranging for off-site events such as training courses or conferences?

[?] Does your company pension scheme provide for spouses? Does this extend to stable partnerships outside marriage?

[?] Do you fund private medical care, including spouses? Does this extend to stable partnerships outside marriage?

13

Language and culture

Cultural pitfalls

In a multilingual, multicultural environment there are three potentially recurring problems:

● misunderstanding

● stereotyping

● the 'halo' effect.

Misunderstanding can arise simply from a mistranslation from another language, but more often it is due to a misreading of the nuance of language. In dealing with people, we put our own interpretation on words or phrases that might mean something subtly different to the speaker. We understand, for example, that there is no single word in French for empowerment as it is commonly used in the United Kingdom or in America, and the French word 'formation' has no English equivalent: it is often loosely translated as training. Whereas an English person is hungry, a French person has hunger (j'ai faim). A simple difference, but of a kind that is prolific and in some cases can cause misunderstanding.

It is very easy to assume that because a person has a particular colour, or accent or infirmity, that he is untrustworthy, or miserly or incapable of doing a particular job. There is all too often ignorance about cultural factors. Racial intolerance abounds throughout the world and organizations must guard against behaviour and attitudes that can amount to 'institutional racism' (*see* Chapter 17).

We can also misinterpret the way people behave by making assumptions about their motivation. You must remember that motivation drives vary from person to person in different cultures and at different stages in their lives. In some countries there are marked differences between the people living in the cities and those in the countryside (for example in Arab countries), and between people from different tribes (for example in parts of Africa). In some countries there has been a marked veneration of age, so that old people are naturally regarded as important and treated with respect, whereas in other countries this is virtually absent.

▶ **There is all too often ignorance about cultural factors**

The young man, a highly successful entrepreneur, was making his first trip to Japan. Alan was importing vast quantities of components from Japan and felt that the time had come to see his agent and his suppliers and to talk business face to face. He arrived at Tokyo airport but was surprised to find that the agent became agitated, looking over Alan's shoulder. The embarrassed agent asked Alan if he had come with his father. He was not looking forward to introducing Alan to other businesspeople in a country where age and seniority were so important. These Japanese businessmen had never met such a young entrepreneur. Commenting on this experience afterwards, Alan Sugar said of the agent: 'He couldn't get to grips with a businessman in his mid-20s.' This event occurred 20 or so years ago, but the point is still relevant.

See Thomas, 1990, p. 59.

In an individual, any cultural background may be overlaid by education and other experiences such as working for a long time for a large firm with a strong culture of its own. In the Solomon Islands there are young people who have been educated in western countries, but who have gone back to work with their friends and families in their own tribes. Their behaviour will differ markedly from that of young people who have not had this 'westernizing' experience: they have made an invaluable contribution to the development of the local communities.

In the absence of any data to the contrary or knowledge about people's cultural norms, we tend to think that people will react to situations as we would ourselves. In practice, the way people react to various situations may be quite different to the ways we would expect on that basis and this can and does cause serious misunderstandings.

> **'The fact is that police officers** who are involved in family liaison must accept a bereaved family as they find it. By that we mean that the way in which a black family reacts to a tragedy such as this may well be different from the reaction of a white family. It is the business of the police to ensure that they fit in with the customs and behaviour of those to whom they are attached for family liaison purposes. Otherwise the relationship is doomed from the start.'
>
> *See* MacPherson, 1999, paragraph 43.8

Stereotyping arises when we assume that an individual will have particular norms, values and modes of behaviour because of some feature such as colour, race, nationality, education or upbringing. It can also arise when we observe that someone has a disability. We can make assumptions about that person's ability that turn out to be totally inaccurate. Studies have shown that even within a cultural group there are quite marked deviations from the dominant pattern of norms, values and behaviours on the part of a very large proportion of the people involved. Thus an individual must be judged not by the colour of his skin, his creed, his nationality or his accent. We must take people as we find them – but at the same time beware of the 'halo effect'.

This so-called 'halo effect' is very powerful. We tend to form strong impressions of a person at the first meeting. We are influenced by the person's appearance, her speech, her dress, her mannerisms, the interest she displays in particular topics and so forth. That initial impression can be so strong that when data comes along that contradicts our first impressions we tend to discount the new data, or to re-interpret the data to fit in with the mental picture of the person we have previously formed. In some cultures

(Japan and Asia) a go-between can be used in business negotiations to minimize this effect.

Our first impressions can be quite wrong, and as long as we hang on to them we can be guilty of misjudging that person. We need to take time and to collect evidence in making judgements about people. Of course, sometimes the data reinforces our intuition. In a foreign country, useful insights can often be obtained by noting how the individual's national peers and colleagues react. Are they diffident, respectful, or guarded towards that individual? If you overreact on the basis of your first impressions, this could damage future relationships.

> **We tend to form strong impressions of a person at the first meeting**

It is very easy to misinterpret the sentiment being expressed by a non-native English speaker. Some nationalities speak English with an abruptness that to an English ear sounds rude or arrogant or with a flippancy that sounds off-hand, when neither is intended.

Later in this chapter we will seek to throw some light on the differences between cultures. The insights from our experiences are supplemented by the work of people such as Trompenaars and Hampden-Turner (1997) or Hofstede (1996), and by extensive discussions with colleagues who have worked with people in different countries and cultures.

Language

If we are to understand other people we must first learn to listen to what they say, then learn to understand where they are coming from so that we can work out the true meaning of their words. Finally we must learn to respect their viewpoints, even if their ideas and their cultural norms are different to our own. In organizations where there is more than one native language and/or cultural background, it is vital to appreciate the communication problems that will arise. Misunderstanding can occur from small nuances in the language.

In many international bodies it is customary for the interpreters to interpret into their native language so that they can give the sense of the message with the appropriate nuances. Where several languages are being used the interpreter may be unable to work directly from the language being spoken, and she will listen in to the interpretation into a language she can understand. This double translation offers more opportunities for misunderstanding. In such meetings it is helpful if the speakers can minimize the use of colloquial terms that often give rise to difficulty in translation. Interpretation can be time-consuming and the interpreter can interfere with the train of thought.

In some industries, English is the preferred language and it is used within the industry throughout the world, for example in the major pharmaceutical and financial organizations. Although much business is conducted internally in this language, there is a need for translations to be provided when dealing with the general public in each area. As English is now widely regarded as the language of commerce, people in many countries are studying the language, but in the American form. Beware of subtle differences from the British version.

Culture

It is worthwhile spending a few minutes thinking about what we mean by culture. The term itself can mean subtly different things in different languages and ethnic settings.

In an organization the culture has been defined as 'the way we do things around here'. But within organizations the culture in particular areas can be very strong and differ markedly from the culture in other areas. There can be a significant difference between the cultures of people in sales and people in engineering, for example. Culture is not something outside our normal experience or an extraneous factor that does not matter. It underpins all that people do and say. We are all, to a large extent, creatures of the culture that we grew up in and live in at the present time. But we may react against that culture in some aspects, and conform in others. Indeed, there is usually more than one culture that we experience. For many people the culture at home is very different to that at work, and different again to that we experience in any religious, leisure or community organizations to which we belong.

> ▶ For many people the culture at home is very different to that at work

Some years ago one of us visited a cigarette factory where people with different grades and jobs wore different coloured uniforms or overalls. There were different grades of canteens and restaurants, with silver service on a polished mahogany table for the directors' lunch. There were even four different grades of toilet, with separate hand towels for each director (on hooks with nameplates) in their own toilet. (There were no women directors!) Every manager had his own office.

On visiting a chocolate factory a few weeks later there was only one restaurant where the managing director queued with everyone else, no separate toilets for different grades of staff, and only one car park where priority was given on the basis of need, not grade. Managers had desks but no separate offices. The managing director was the only person who had a separate office and the walls were of glass from waist height up. He wore a white coat like everybody else and had his first name on the outside of the pocket.

In the UK civil service there was a time when you could tell the seniority of an individual by the cut of his carpet.

You can observe the behaviour of people who belong to a particular culture. This behaviour is based to a considerable extent on the norms and values of the cultural group. Norms have been defined in terms of the way people normally behave. You may be in an organization where every man in the office wears a collar and tie – or one in which nobody does! Generally speaking a newcomer in such an organization will look at the other people and conform to their dress code, not out of any value or belief but because he does not particularly want to stand out in the crowd. Of course, there will be the individual who does want to be noticed, and he may wear a bright tie or an open collar.

People who work in laboratories generally wear protective clothing, not because everybody else does, but because they believe it is the safe and sensible thing to do. One advantage is that if your clothing is damaged, it will be the overall, not your best suit. There is a value system at work here – the belief that it is better to be safe than sorry.

Thus some behaviour arises from norms, and other behaviour from values from cultural influences and socialization. Perhaps the most striking difference in values held by different cultures is about loyalty. Do you think one should be more loyal to one's friend or to the law? If your friend commits a serious crime, do you report him to the authorities, or keep quiet? In some cultures, loyalty to one's friend is more important than loyalty to the law of the land. This is, of course, even stronger if, for any reason, you have no respect for the actual laws in question. You may answer that this is a matter of degree. Precisely – but when a real situation arises people will react differently, based in part on these cultural differences. If you are an individual with a strong sense of loyalty to the laws and rules, you may be surprised when a colleague takes a totally different attitude.

Underlying these norms and values there is a set of assumptions that people share in a culture, and these beliefs have a profound influence on the norms and values of the society. Often such assumptions are not open to question, but they are changing: quickly in some societies, slower in others. If you keep on asking why, eventually you will get the answer, because that is the way it is – then you are probably in the realm of assumptions. Often these are unspoken and unnoticed, yet they have a profound influence on the daily lives of the people involved.

> **Underlying these norms and values there are a set of assumptions**

If an individual assumes that someone will perform better because she comes from a better family, or from a better university, or has more years of experience, he will not easily be moved from that belief. You may say, but what of the evidence? As a matter of fact, in societies where such assumptions hold sway they often, for a variety of reasons, become a self-fulfilling prophecy. Such people, on average, actually do well!

The subject is too large to deal with in any depth here, but the following remarks may help you to gain some insights that will help you through this difficult area of people management. The ways in which culture can influence people's attitudes and behaviour are summarized below. Remember that there will be considerable variation from the central values outlined in each case.

Managing cultural diversity means taking account of these differences and finding ways in which people with different norms and values can learn to respect one another and work constructively together. The key to success lies in first recognizing that differences exist and seeking to identify the key ones, then finding a modus operandi that seizes upon the fact that in most cases you can find a way to make one value or approach complement another, drawing strength from both. It is impossible to give hard and fast advice about how to deal with every situation, but some clues are given in the text below.

Relationships

A number of cultural factors can be grouped together under this general heading. How ready are we to bend the rules to preserve and foster relationships? How highly do we rate the community compared with our individual importance? To what extent should we be prepared to be open with our feelings and reactions to people and events? How close should we get to the people we work with on a personal level?

Rules and relationships: in some cultures, people place more importance on relationships with others than on the rules and laws that are laid down. Where you encounter this, take time to develop relationships, and be prepared to supplement rational arguments with the development of trust.

In Berlin it used to be rare to see someone crossing the road against a red light, even when there was not a vehicle in sight, but in Rome most people seem to ignore the traffic signals. In Brussels (a truly international city) you will see all kinds of behaviour at the pedestrian crossings! But tourism is levelling behaviour, for the more people travel, the more behaviour patterns tend to become more uniform. At busy times in London's Oxford Street, police with megaphones have to stop tourists throwing themselves under buses at road junctions.

Typically in Switzerland, the USA, the UK or Canada, for example, the norm is for people to obey the rules, but in Venezuela, South Korea, Russia and India friendships matter more than the rulebook. In dealing with people from the latter countries you may find that a flexible contract that enables people to get results with dignity is better than one that tries to specify the last jot and tittle. The Swiss, on the other hand, may prefer precision.

When he arrived for his first meeting at a European Committee in Brussels, it was interesting to note that some people arrived early or on time, typically the British, the Irish and the Germans, whereas people of certain other nationalities (that we shall not name to avoid giving offence!) were not in their seats by the appointed hour. As the meeting started late, however, most people were present at the start. His first reaction was to be annoyed to be kept waiting, but after a time he became accustomed to the style, although he still regularly turned up on time.

As circumstances change, people in the USA or Canada might expect employees or suppliers to stick to previously agreed contracts, but in India or the Arab countries the expectation is that as the situation changes, the contracts can be varied to take account of these factors. We are talking about unilateral action that seems reasonable to the person who makes the change. If you are from the USA and find that someone in another country is not adhering to your contract as laid down, ask for an explanation, be reasonable and seek to renegotiate a mutually acceptable deal, based on the changed circumstances. If you are from a country where you feel free to vary the conditions of a contract in the light of changed circumstances, be warned that your business partner in the contract may not see this in the same way. The advice is the same – renegotiate. Long-term planning as seen through western eyes may, at times, be conceived as totally unrealistic – and perhaps a little ridiculous.

Be very cautious about admiring objects (for example a watch or a piece of jewellery) belonging to an Arab executive or official. He may feel obliged to offer it to you as a gift (even if he can't afford it), and to refuse will cause offence.

The individual and the group: in some cultures, people regard the cohesion and achievement of the group as more important than the exultation of any individual member. Do not allow yourself to become frustrated when you observe this behaviour. Be patient in developing goals and rewards to which people will respond, ensuring that the value and the achievements of the group are recognized as well as those of individuals.

In Canada, the UK and the USA people aspire to individual freedom and achievement, whereas in France and Brazil people appear to have a stronger commitment to the community. Rewarding people who do well as individuals appears to be a strong force at the current time in the UK and the USA. All too often the system breaks down because (a) the situation changes and the rules set up to measure achievement become obsolete and (b) the achievement of results can rarely be attributed to one individual alone. In many societies it is seen as a bit silly to think in these terms, and the need is to develop and mobilize the whole group and the whole community and to share the rewards accordingly.

This does not rule out some differentiation in the rewards attributed to individuals, but it does recognize that in most situations people actually depend on each other for success. In countries such as Egypt, Mexico and Japan you can find that the importance of developing an individual's skills resides in the contribution that person can make to the community, rather than simply to herself as an individual.

Expressing feelings: in some cultures, people think it is important to demonstrate one's feelings freely, but others believe that feelings should not be displayed openly. If you are not used to such outward displays, learn to accept the demonstration of people's feelings, but be careful in interpreting people's behaviour.

We communicate with each other not only with words and sentences but also by looks, gestures and even the tone of voice that we use. It is important to seek to identify all these signs. (In using e-mails, some people have sought to overcome the lack of non-verbal signals by using smileys and emoticons.)

Furthermore there are conventions that often we observe unconsciously, unless they are contravened. In Anglo-Saxon cultures we expect to be able to finish a sentence before someone else starts to talk, and we may even consider it rude when we are interrupted, although radio and television interviewers have tended to erode this convention. In Latin countries, such an interruption is more likely to signify that the person who interrupts is interested in what the speaker has to say. In Arab countries, the telephone will be answered even in the middle of a delicate negotiation. No insult is intended.

> ▶ **We communicate by looks, gestures and tone of voice**

Arabs are tactile (men with men, women with women, but never between the sexes), with much touching of elbows, double handshakes and occasionally embraces. This is done without the least sense of impropriety or embarrassment. It is usually best to accept this behaviour with good grace, but not to take the initiative.

Whereas in Anglo-Saxon cultures it is generally welcomed if a speaker changes his tone of voice in dramatic bursts to make his speech more colourful, in Latin cultures this tonal variation is much more frequent, and in oriental cultures it is less pronounced. In African cultures, to raise one's voice may be regarded as a demonstration of concern, but in Asian countries 'shouting' may be regarded as a loss of control and hence a loss of face. In the West we are brought up to fill silences – feel uncomfortable if nobody is speaking – but in the Arab world it is quite acceptable to sit together in silence for minutes at a time.

Coping with involvement: in some cultures, people like to be closely involved with those they do business with, but others like to 'keep their distance'. If you come from a culture that respects 'distance', learn to consider the wider picture of the person, his interests and his experience before judging behaviour that seems illogical, and structure your interactions carefully, but allowing time for people to develop ideas and improvements.

Status, time and nature

Another set of culture factors is related to the following questions. On what basis do we rate people and reward them? How do we view time? For everyday affairs, what is our planning time horizon? How important is it to be 'on time'? Do we want to gain mastery of nature and to be in charge of our personal and corporate destiny, if necessary to work directly against the forces around us, or do we want to adapt to our circumstances and work with the pressures we encounter? In each case the answer cannot be a straight yes or no, but a matter of degree.

Status issues: in some cultures, people ascribe status to those who achieve results, especially recent results, but in other cultures status is accorded on the basis of age, experience, family background or education. Be prepared to respect local cultural norms and, where appropriate, show respect in accordance with the culture, and give space to people who have seniority and/or achievement to their credit. Be very careful about reward and promotion systems, and other related 'influence factors'.

▶ **Be prepared to respect local cultural norms**

In the USA, Canada, Ireland and the UK, individuals are, on the whole, recognized and rewarded for their achievements in the world of work, whereas in the Arab countries and Asia, recognition and reward may depend much more upon such factors as age, gender, social connections, education and profession. In France, the graduates of the *Grandes Écoles* are very highly regarded, and in Italy older people are generally venerated. If you show disrespect for age in an Italian culture you may pay a price for that, for example in a negotiating situation.

In the copper belt in Zambia, before copper was extracted, among four or five tribal groups there was a social and cultural hierarchy, with one group being recognized as leaders and highly respected by other tribes. In the very early days when western companies moved in and set up mining operations and factories, if management did not recognize this in the way they organized the workforce, problems would ensue. For example, a personnel manager from the 'wrong' tribal grouping would find it difficult to cope with people pressures from his own family tribe, let alone from the other tribes. It was necessary to appoint in supervisory positions, people from the tribal background recognised as having the tribal status and authority to get things done.

In some cultures women find it particularly difficult to gain recognition and status, but this situation is changing – albeit slowly – in many countries. Watch out for status symbols – the size of the office or carpet (British civil service) or the size of desk (in Arab countries).

Concepts of time: in some cultures, time is regarded as linked, with the past and prospective future being regarded as an important part of the current situation, whereas in other cultures the emphasis is on the here and now, planning only for the immediate future. Furthermore, in some cultures activities are viewed as a sequence of events that must be completed on time, and in others activities are best interwoven with several conducted concurrently: relationships here take precedence over time schedules. These perspectives are not difficult to reconcile once you recognize that they exist. You need to be patient with people who want to look at relevant past events and to seek to work out what might happen in the longer term as proposals are considered.

You must recognize that some people will want meetings to start on time and others will give more importance to maintaining relationships, even if this means being late. Respect for the other person's position is vital for effective collaboration. In Arab countries you should arrive on time yourself, but not be offended if the other party is late.

Many of us are accustomed to think of time as an ongoing but disconnected sequence of minute intervals. We live in the ever-present 'now', regarding the past as lost and gone, and seeking to make decisions for the future based on the best data we have, recognizing that it is often inadequate. Generally speaking, we plan precisely for the next few minutes and less precisely the further we look into the distance. We may regard it as efficient to plan to go directly from the start to the destination by the shortest route, the 'critical path'. There is something to be said, however, for doing a number of tasks at the same time, or rather flitting from one to another, such that the main task may take longer, but many other tasks are achieved within that same time span. When drawing up a business plan we must always bear in mind the need to update and modify this when circumstances change.

Whenever a few British people want to do the same thing (board a bus, buy a ticket), they spontaneously form a queue, but in other cultures people just hang about and seek their chance to board or buy. The British have a strong sense of sequence. Other cultures may see life as a series of circles, bringing us back to the same point (morning and evening, spring and summer, life and death). The rush of western civilization has no place in quiet Asian meditation. It may be better to follow where circumstances lead than to strive to follow preconceived plans.

One of the features of this time perception is the way people in some cultures (USA, UK) want to go straight to the point and limit their analysis to what seems at first sight to be relevant, whereas in other cultures (for example in France) people want to set each point and each decision into a context that may include the past as well as the present.

For a time one of us represented the United Kingdom in committee meetings in Brussels and in Berlin. When he listened to the speeches of the French representatives he was astonished to find that they seemed to go all around the world to make a point. As he listened more carefully, however, he realized that the French speakers always sought to put the point they wished to make in its context. So they would mention how the situation had arisen and the circumstances in which it was set. Then the point was made, clearly. The more he got to know French officials as friends and colleagues and to understand their way of thinking, the more he learned to respect this approach. He was later engaged in a number of projects working closely and effectively alongside French experts.

There is a place for all these approaches to time and the management of events, recognizing the insights that each approach can bring to our organizations. This becomes more acute as organizations trade globally and the world becomes 'smaller'.

Go with the flow: in some cultures, people seek to take control of nature and of the events that shape their lives, but in other cultures people try to work out how to 'go with the flow', to work with nature and to fit into the stream of life, to seize the moment, not to create it. The tendency to respect nature, culture and the environment is gaining ground. Finding the way forward without winning at the expense of other people or the environment is the key. Get as near as you can to the win-win situation, not the win-lose.

> ▶ Some people like to think of themselves as in charge of their own destiny!

In the UK and the USA, people like to think of themselves as in charge of their own destiny, battling against the forces of nature to achieve their goals, and competing with other people to gain the mastery of the marketplace. But in Venezuela, China and Nepal there is an acceptance of the overwhelming forces of nature and the need to find ways and means of working within that context and achieving your aims, within reason, by harnessing and adapting to these forces.

Corporate cultures

One of the problems you will face is that there are probably significant variations in the cultures in different sections of your own organization. Many of us are familiar with the potential conflict between an engineering department wanting to get at machines for maintenance that the production department wants to run into the ground, and marketing people who expect manufacturing plants to change products at the drop of a hat. In part, these frustrations arise because of differences in the culture of the departments.

It is also possible to explore the culture of your own organization using the parameters explained in this chapter, but the problem is that by the time you have the answer, the organization will have moved on and you will be looking at history. Incidentally, the method you used to measure the culture has also, most likely, changed it. In one sense it is helpful that cultures can change, because organizations need to adapt to changing circumstances, and to respond to changing pressures.

> ▶ **The method you use to measure culture is very likely to change it**

If you find that you need to accommodate several of these cultural factors in your organization, you will need to develop a corporate culture that is (a) sensitive to these differences, and (b) where people learn to value difference and to build upon it.

As we have seen from the examples, in most cases it is quite possible to reconcile differences of approach, but when there are differences in cultural behaviour, then understanding and tolerance are the only answers, although these are difficult in practice. If you ask people from one culture to work in another, or to manage people with a significantly different culture, for example in your own country, you should provide training to help them to acquire the sensitivity and management skills they need.

A word of caution: we cannot stress too strongly two factors: people do not behave exactly according to the norms of their culture, and these norms are changing as we write. The above remarks are to help you think about the subject, they do not provide a simplistic formula for you to follow.

Progress checklist

?   Do you know the extent of the cultural diversity in your organization? Have you considered the potential pitfalls and problems you might encounter?

?   What languages do your people speak and write? Are you confident that you have minimized the potential for misunderstanding?

?   Have you grasped the essence of what culture means in your context?

?   Are your managers equipped to deal with the diversified characteristics and approaches they may encounter in relationships?

?   Are you likely to confront problems where employees – or suppliers or customers – have different concepts of status, time or the use of nature that you may need to take into account?

?   Are you developing a corporate culture that is sensitive to socio-cultural issues and flexible enough to use them to advantage?

14

Managing disability

The impact of disability

Managing diversity means, among other things, enabling people who have some form of disability to make their full contribution to the organization. You must never think of or talk of a person primarily in terms of his disability. He is, first and foremost, a person. He is not that deaf chap, but a person with hearing difficulties. She is not that blind woman, but a person with visual impairment. The disability is a challenge to be met, overcome and managed. It is your problem, not just that of the employee or job applicant with the impairment.

It is difficult for people without disabilities to fully appreciate the problems of people who have disabilities. They are thought of as 'different' whereas they see themselves as normal people who have some area of disability. For this reason some companies (for example British Telecom) have introduced the concept of a 'disability champion'. In some cases they have appointed a person with a disability to perform this role. These companies have found that such a champion can talk to people who have problems and see the company and management through their eyes.

The term disability covers many different conditions. We tend to think automatically about people with mobility, sight or hearing problems. But there are also those with literacy and numeracy problems (including dyslexia), and those who suffer from epilepsy and other disorders who may need special provisions to enable them to function effectively in your organization. For monitoring purposes it is helpful to define a person as having a disability if he has an impairment with a substantial impact, say for a year or more. Effects that are not long term, such as a broken limb that should recover within 12 months, are not included.

▶ **The term disability covers many different conditions**

By disability we mean a physical or mental impairment that may have an impact on the person's ability to carry out normal day-to-day activities. Mental impairment relates to a wide range of mental functions, including learning disabilities or poor memory. Abilities required for normal day-to-day activities include speech, hearing, eyesight, the sense of touch, mobility, manual dexterity, physical co-ordination, continence, ability to lift, carry or move everyday objects, memory, concentration, learning, understanding and the perception of the risk of physical danger. If a person wears glasses or contact lenses and this enables him to lead a normal life, this is not regarded as a disability. A severe disfigurement can be regarded as a disability – provided this is not a tattoo or non-medical body piercing.

Sciatica can sometimes cause people to lose the sense of touch in the feet. We heard of an individual who was unable to detect sensations through his feet, and could not feel how hard he was pressing the brake pedal in his car. The loss of such sensations can also be dangerous if an individual is unable to feel pain, for example when she is near a fire.

In many countries there are laws that compel employers to avoid discrimination and to provide facilities for disabled people. These laws normally apply specifically to recruitment and dismissal procedures as well as to discrimination in general.

As a responsible employer you should ensure that you do not directly or indirectly discriminate in respect of the:

- recruitment procedures
- terms and conditions of employment
- opportunities for advancement, including training
- dismissal procedures.

Sometimes the disability becomes so profound that the individual is no longer able to do a proper job. In such cases the person may be dismissed, provided every effort has been made to accommodate the person's disability by all reasonable adjustments.

For some years BT has had a positive policy on valuing ability and employing disabled people in ways that make a positive contribution to the company. A young woman who is deaf has worked for BT for 18 years. She communicates with her colleagues by lip reading and sign language. A senior analyst programmer who is blind has worked for BT for 16 years. His PC is adapted to convert his screen work to Braille. This allows him access to mainframes and e-mail. He tapes the meetings he attends and takes notes in Braille. A planner who is a wheelchair user has worked at BT for 15 years. These are some examples of the way BT has effectively employed talented people in spite of their disabilities.

The BT Equal Opportunities Steering Group is led by the managing directors of the key business units and brings together senior managers for every business unit. It clearly exercises a very powerful influence on BT's policies and practices in this area.

BT has also instituted a special post of 'disability champion', arranges disability roadshows, known as AccessAbility Roadshows, has an internal disabled employee network, Able2, and publishes a special newsletter for those with an interest in disabled people in the organization. Like many organizations, BT recognizes the value of networks and promotes, for example, a Deaf Awareness Network. It also conducts surveys and publishes the results internally. BT's 'Age and Disability Unit' is dedicated, among other things, to helping people with a disability to use the telephone.

Moving about

Getting about can be a problem for people with defective sight and hearing, as well as people with mobility problems. People who have difficulty reading may also have problems getting around complicated buildings and new surroundings. Consider the access to your premises and people's ability to move around freely. Is there wheelchair access – ramps and wide doorways? Can a wheelchair user move about freely? What measures can you take to assist her to leave the building in the case of a fire or other emergency? Are there toilet provisions for wheelchair users? Can doors be readily opened with one hand? Are reception desks at a suitable height for wheelchair users?

Your organization may have buildings that cannot be readily adapted for wheelchair users. This should not, however, discourage you from considering employing disabled people. In the UK, only 6 per cent of disabled people with severe disabilities require a wheelchair for movement. You can employ disabled people who do not require wheelchairs while you set realistic targets for when wheelchair access can be achieved, enabling you to offer access to more disabled people, whether employees, customers or suppliers.

To move about freely people must be able to follow the signposting, particularly for the emergency exits. For the benefit of people with literacy problems it is important to use exit signs that are word-free. Many partially sighted people need help in negotiating steps: the edges need to be clearly marked. Some people with mobility problems may not be confined to a wheelchair, but need the support of handrails, especially on the stair cases and even when there are just one or two steps to negotiate. Blind people often have the help of guide dogs. Are your premises friendly towards them? Do glass doors have wording or artwork so that they can be clearly seen by partially sighted people?

▶ **Are your premises user-friendly towards people with disabilities?**

If you have an old building, some modifications may be too extensive and expensive to incorporate and compromises may be needed between the ideal and the practical. We have encountered a number of organizations where modifications to old buildings are impractical, but where new premises are being designed to facilitate the movement and safety of people with disabilities.

People who have limited mobility may find it difficult to get quickly to a telephone. Cordless and mobile phones are a real help in such cases. An alternative in some situations is simply to extend the wire. Someone with mobility difficulties may also have problems calling for help in an emergency. One possible solution is an alarm system with a body-worn trigger.

Special car parking spaces for disabled people are now commonplace. You will need to consider the needs of your employees and your visitors when planning your organization's car parking provisions.

Vision

Many people with limited or zero eyesight lead highly successful lives, and make a major contribution to our society. A number of aids are now available, including Braille keyboards. You will need to consider the kinds of work that can be undertaken in your organization by a person with these difficulties and make appropriate provision.

Guide dogs can assist blind people in a number of ways – opening and closing doors, switching lights on and off, picking up dropped items, calling a lift, pressing a pedestrian crossing button, emptying the washing machine, and much more. These skills can materially assist a blind person in the workplace, and this should be borne in mind in the design of the workstation.

Many blind people find it easier to use the modern press-button telephones with memories, and if the number 5 is distinguished e.g. with a raised dot, they can learn to use the buttons. If the letters are large, partially sighted people can often see them. A classified directory service is available by telephone for blind people unable to use the printed telephone directories. There are also telephone answering machines that give an audible sound when there are messages to be played.

Hearing and speech

People who have hearing difficulties are particularly vulnerable when an alarm bell sounds, for example the fire alarm. In some cases it may be possible to arrange for visual warnings to be given at the same time, or to ensure that the person with a hearing difficulty is always working near other people who will hear the alarm and alert him.

In some organizations volunteers receive training in sign language so that they can more effectively communicate with deaf colleagues. It is particularly helpful if some members of management are prepared to accept such training.

For those who are hard of hearing it is possible to obtain telephones with a ringer volume control and to vary the pitch of the ring. Extension bells can be fitted. For those who cannot hear at all it is possible to have visual signals or vibrating pagers. It is possible to increase the sound volume reaching the telephone earpiece with speech amplifiers, and these can be linked to inductive couplers. Portable amplifiers can be obtained for use with unamplified telephones. You should also ensure that if you have emergency telephones in the lifts, these can be inductively coupled to a hearing aid. For the totally deaf there are text phones (with a keyboard and screen), fax machines and videophones.

Some people have difficulty in speaking, perhaps because they have a quiet voice, or no voice at all, or their speech is unclear. People who suffer from deafness often have problems with speaking as well and have to receive special training. For those with partial speech loss there are special telephones with outgoing speech amplifiers. Those without speech may use speech synthesizers, text phones, type-talk services or facsimile machines to communicate via the telephone line.

▶ **You may need to help your managers and other workers to learn patience!**

We often fail to realize just how isolating it can be to suffer from partial or total deafness. People frequently lose patience with those who have hearing difficulties and regard them as unintelligent, when all that has happened is that they cannot hear the conversation properly and hence cannot comment in a timely fashion. If you have people with these difficulties it may not be enough simply to provide hearing aids and amplifying earphones. You may need to help your managers and other workers to learn patience! You might consider engaging the help of trained 'signers' until some of your own volunteers have learned to use sign language.

Companies with an intranet have considered the setting up of special pages on the web to provide information for deaf people on how to obtain special equipment, how to book an interpreter, and how to display finger spelling on the web. The site can also be used to help members of the workforce to communicate with deaf people, for example lip reading, sign language and simply writing things down.

Literacy problems

A person with severe literacy problems will find it difficult to work in a typical workplace surrounded by written signs. For this reason it is now customary to use pictures wherever possible to denote such things as exits and hazards. Dyslexia, or word blindness, can be a hindrance in, for example, using word-processing software. However, modern software with spellchecking included can be a material help to those with this problem.

An article appeared in *The Times* in London on 8 November 1999 under the heading 'Dyslexic wins payout over spelling failure'. It reported that a major catering company had been ordered to pay a dyslexic former employee nearly £6,500 because she was forced to leave her job. At the employment tribunal she had claimed that her employer was unsympathetic towards her difficulty with spelling and had refused to buy a £23 spellchecker for her to use at work. The tribunal was told that the Dyslexic Institute had recommended the purchase of spellcheck software and tuition. The cost would not exceed £220 and would have enabled her to do her work to a satisfactory standard.

Manual dexterity

Some operations, notably using the telephone or a keyboard, require a degree of manual dexterity. For people who cannot readily hold a telephone and make notes, for example, there are telephones with amplifiers that enable you to use them hands free, and it is possible to obtain headrests, headsets or handset holders. There are also a number of aids that can help people to grasp objects.

Recruitment and redeployment

People with disabilities are unlikely to apply for jobs at your organization if they do not see it as welcoming. Some organizations publicize their openness to such applications and ensure that any recruitment agencies they employ are fully aware of this policy. Job advertisements and application forms should not imply that a person might not get the job because they have a disability, or that the employer is unwilling to make reasonable adjustments to employment arrangements or to premises.

You must ensure that when you call a person with a disability for interview you have made proper arrangements for access and for communicating effectively with the applicant. As indicated above, there are a number of steps you can take to facilitate access and communications. In drawing up your selection criteria, ensure these are not applied in a way that may be considered discriminatory. It might be helpful, for example, if the applicant has a valid driving licence, but it may not be essential for the job in question.

When a job applicant with a disability can clearly do the job – with reasonable modifications to your working practices and work allocation – then be prepared to make these modifications and not to reject the person because of the necessary adjustments. If one of your employees becomes disabled, explore the help you can give her to continue in the job, and if this is not possible consider reallocating work so that she can retain some of her responsibilities. If this is not possible, search for a possible reallocation of duties that will enable her to continue to make a valuable contribution to the organization. If you decide that new equipment is needed or new tasks are needed, be sure to arrange for appropriate training.

Respect for people

Many of the barriers that people with disabilities face in the employment scene are the direct result of the negative attitudes and misconceptions held by society. Small details of language and behaviour reinforce these attitudes. By encouraging positive language and behaviour, managers can begin to redress the balance (*see* Table 14.1).

If you find that a significant proportion of your staff persist in using words and behaviour that are offensive to people with disabilities, you might use Table 14.1 as the basis of some short awareness seminars.

Table 14.1 Respect for people with disabilities

Avoid words such as 'handicapped'.	Refer to people with disabilities.
Don't classify people with medical labels.	Many people do not conform to the stereotypes suggested by these labels.
Do not refer to an individual as if she is a 'condition'.	Refer to her as a person with epilepsy, not as an 'epileptic'.
Avoid words that invite pity, or that imply frailty or dependence, phrases such as 'crippled by', 'suffering from', 'afflicted by' or 'a victim of'.	Talk instead about this person who has hearing difficulties, or about a person with cerebral palsy.
Do not refer to an individual as mentally handicapped when you mean someone with learning difficulties.	Do not confuse mental illness with learning problems.
Do not refer to someone as 'an invalid', wheelchair bound or confined to a wheelchair.	Describe such an individual as a wheelchair user or a person who uses a wheelchair.

Progress checklist

[?] Have you considered how to encourage your employees to treat people with disabilities as 'normal' people?

[?] Can people with mobility problems get around your premises?

[?] Do you have a target date by which time your premises will be accessible to wheelchair users?

[?] Have you made adequate provision for any visually impaired people in your employment?

[?] Do you have positive policies and a supportive culture that help people with hearing or speech problems to play a full part in your organization?

[?] Have you demonstrated your openness to applications from disabled people and made proper arrangements for the interview situation?

[?] Have you set target dates by which time your premises will be user-friendly towards people with disabilities?

15

Management learning

▶ Secure commitment and example at the top

▶ Identify the key learning needs

▶ Align attitude, behaviour and vocabulary

▶ Train all new managers and supervisors to manage within a diverse workforce

▶ Create a culture of mutual support in the implementation of diversity policies

Start at the top

The management of diversity requires the establishment of some very clear policies at the highest level in the organization, coupled with the development of consistent procedures for dealing with people. Unless your organization is ahead of the field, steps may need to be taken to ensure that managers, recruiters and trainers fully appreciate the implications of managing within a diverse labour force, and the behaviours required to achieve success.

As the 'top team' in the organization grapples with these policies and practices, a learning process is taking place. It is wise to have the help of an experienced facilitator during this process, unless the team is mature enough to work effectively on such problems and has, within its members, the expertise required to develop the policies and their implementation. In our experience very senior people, for example a board of directors, will not take kindly to any suggestion that they need training. Indeed, few trainers could undertake such a task without wasting the time of the board. But if the group is prepared to spend some time together to thrash out these issues, a skilled facilitator can help to ensure that they do not waste time, and that they come to an understanding and agreement about what needs to be done.

This is an issue where it will not do to simply nod through bits of paper with policies written on them. One method that has been used with some success is to list a number of awkward questions that you put to the top team to consider and debate. These can include questions such as: How soon do we expect to have a significant number of women or black people in senior management and on the board? What changes will we need to make to the way we operate if we have more women here? What steps should we take to enable more black people to attain the standards required to reach higher management positions? What sort of image do we have with our employees, and our customers? Do we want to make it easy for gay people to be open about their sexuality? How do we expect the workforce to react? How will we react? Do we want to encourage older people to work here? How will this affect promotion prospects for younger people in our organization?

▶ Managers, recruiters and trainers must learn how to manage a diverse workforce

Choose questions that are relevant to your organization, and questions that will grab the attention of senior people because they will have an impact on the way the organization is managed. The positive gains to the organization need to be identified and stressed. Any problems related to conformity to the law or matters of contract compliance will need to be fully considered. In some countries, for example, government contracts may be conditional on meeting some aspect of diversity management. Sometimes government departments or government-funded bodies also have instructions to comply with diversity issues. We understand that in 1999, health service trusts in the UK were instructed to reflect in their employees the racial mix in the areas that they serve. The USA affirmative action programme makes demands on organizations that receive contracts. Such factors will form an essential element in senior management discussions.

Assemble some data to inform the discussion. Specify the proportion of women, black people and people with disabilities at different levels of management. How does the ratio of black people relate to the population in the area around the site? Note how many incidents of racist remarks or sexual harassment have been reported. How many complaints of discrimination in selections for promotion have been recorded in the past 12 months? Some of the questions should initiate discussion about attitudes and behaviour.

Many organizations have found that the development of codes of behaviour is a useful tool in promoting learning in the context of diversity management. Top management needs to be involved, and including consultation with employees on these issues can, in itself, be a valuable learning experience for managers.

▶ **Assemble some data to inform the discussion**

Codes of practice on empowering people with disabilities, equal opportunities and valuing difference have all proved useful.

Key learning needs

Managers at all levels need to know and understand:

- the organization's policy on diversity
- legal requirements
- any contract compliance issues
- the organization's procedures related to diversity
- how these apply to their area of responsibility.

Some of the issues that need to be highlighted include:

- The positive nature of the management of diversity;
- the benefit to the business from a highly motivated diverse workforce;
- the importance of valuing difference, not merely coping with it;
- that discriminatory practices must be identified and eliminated at every stage in the employment relationship;
- the requirement to identify and acknowledge every instance of bullying and harassment and to deal with it constructively;
- the organization's requirement to comply with any laws relating to diversity;
- that diversity management applies to relationships with people outside the organization such as customers and suppliers.

According to the legal requirements and the organizational context, there may be a need to stress certain aspects of diversity in training and development. For example, where a company is situated in an area with a high proportion of Asian people in the population, programmes could include a focus on helping managers to understand the culture of the people concerned so that these factors can be taken into account in forming constructive relationships with both the local community and those Asians who come to work at the company.

In an organization recruiting and promoting women that has hitherto been dominated by men, it may be necessary to place special emphasis on the need to avoid all actions and words that can be seen as sexual discrimination or harassment. Some organizations have specific codes of conduct aimed at preventing harassment at work as a part of their diversity management programmes.

After an introduction, a training course on the prevention of harassment and bullying in the workplace might cover, for example, the following topics:

- the company policy on fair treatment
- the company approach to the prevention of harassment
- how to recognise sexual harassment
- how to recognize racial harassment
- how to determine if behaviour is unwanted
- how to avoid harassment
- how to deal with harassment
- how to respond to a complaint
- responsibilities of managers
- responsibilities of employees
- role and responsibilities of human resource and/or equal opportunity managers.

Where an organization takes steps to employ more disabled people it may be useful for some managers to learn sign language to help them in communicating with deaf people. Managers need to be made aware of the kinds of problems that visually impaired people may meet, and to know how to manage the workplace to take account of this. For example, good housekeeping and clear walkways are essential, and an understanding of the role and abilities of guide dogs and consideration for their welfare is an important part of this management. Carers have particular needs relating to communications and probably to special leave. Managers need to be aware of these needs and company policy in these areas.

There are a number of devices that can enable people with disabilities to cope with a range of tasks, and managers need to be aware of these, as appropriate to the people they employ. Managers will need to understand just what adjustments are considered to be reasonable for helping a person with a disability, whether this is to comply with legislation (in the UK, for example) or with what might well be the broader policy of the firm. Managers must be aware that this policy applies equally to promotions, transfers and training.

Attitudes and behaviour

If you want to bring about real change you will need to attack this on two fronts. First of all you need clear policies and these need to be worked through with managers at all levels to ensure understanding and, hopefully, to secure commitment. To change attitudes requires a mixture of reason and emotion. People must not only see the reasons for the change, for example for more women and black people in senior positions, they must also be convinced that the management is behind the initiative – as demonstrated by example and by the commitment of time and money to a change programme.

▶ **People must be convinced that management is behind the initiative**

Alongside these efforts to change attitudes, managers must learn to adhere to a clear set of rules of behaviour, some enshrined in procedures, but others that evolve as people tackle specific issues. In selection panels, for example, one of the pitfalls is to ask questions that one section of the population is more likely to know about than another – for instance men interested in sport, or people of a particular race or creed. There is probably no deliberate desire to discriminate, but it happens. Another problem is that in different cultures people react differently to the same set of questions. In one culture the candidate will wish to give a clear, simple answer to each question, but a person from another culture will wish to describe the context before answering a specific point. Women may react differently to a line of questioning than men in similar situations.

The organization will need to develop a culture where it is unacceptable to harass or discriminate against any individual on grounds of gender, race, creed, background, personality, sexual orientation, lifestyle, age or disability. The policies and procedures need to be spelt out clearly and communicated to everybody. The implications of these policies must be thought through in every aspect of the work of the organization. Since managers may well be unable to recognize discriminatory behaviour themselves, it must become acceptable for people who feel that they are being harassed or suffering discrimination, and people who see others so treated, to report these observations. Unfortunately, occasions are likely to arise where the manager is unwilling to take the matter seriously, and for this reason alternative routes for reporting such incidents must be introduced.

Men who have been accustomed to managing in an organization where few women reach senior positions and where most people are of the same race can easily slip into a number of actions, words and phrases that others will find offensive. They are also likely to make assumptions that prove to be untrue – that women are illogical, old people can't learn, people of a certain race are unreliable. All this is the very stuff of the prejudice that leads to discrimination, and it must be rooted out. But how can this be achieved?

A small public sector organization had, by tradition, been managed by men in a rather militaristic fashion. Managers gave orders and expected them to be obeyed without question. There were some women in the junior 'ranks' but none had become a manager. A new director was appointed to the unit and she made it her business to ensure that in future competitions for promotion women had a fair chance of success. Over a period of six or seven years the position changed, with some 30 per cent of the managers being female. At first there were problems, but eventually female managers were accepted by both other managers and by the 'lower ranks'. The culture changed and became more open, with people still doing what they were told, but being able to question decisions and seek reasons for particular procedures. It was found that some procedures could be improved and the organization was seen to be more responsive to the people it served.

Management training

A simple course to open up the subject of harassment is given above. However, although it is not easy, one of the key factors to introduce in training programmes is a number of exercises that make managers and supervisors – and even trainers themselves – question their own behaviour and how people susceptible to discrimination will perceive it. Training courses involving role play and role reversal can have a significant impact. It can be helpful to collect information on harassment, bullying and discriminatory behaviour and practices within the organization to illustrate the kinds of words and actions that fall within this area.

Training courses in the form of workshops where people discuss real issues and incidents and how they should be managed are probably the most useful. Such workshops may need a formal element where the local legislation relating to diversity is explained, and where the relevant policies and practice of the organization are outlined. In some cases, for example in dealing with recruitment or selection procedures, more specific training may be required.

It is usually not possible in short workshops or training courses to equip managers with the skills needed to implement these policies and procedures. These events should 'sensitize' managers to the issues and provide insights into the kinds of behaviour that will be expected. But if they are accustomed to managing in ways that conflict with diversity, a short course is unlikely to change their behaviour. Follow-up in the form of coaching and probably counselling may be required. It is often valuable to include in the workshop some training to enable people to engage in co-counselling (see below), where two managers can help each other to improve once they return to the workplace.

> **Learning events can sensitize managers to diversity issues**

Another tool used in these training courses is to present the participants with a number of scenarios. Under the guidance of the tutor, the participants can discuss the issues involved in each incident, various courses of action, possible outcomes and whether the course of action complies with the law and the organization's policy. In this field it is essential to make managers think about examples. Another approach is to describe a situation involving behaviour and to ask participants to classify the behaviour involved as acceptable, inappropriate, discriminatory or harassing.

Examples of such incidents are provided in Table 15.1. (We are indebted to Reuters for permission to use some ideas from their in-house training material as the basis for this table.) Participants will then be asked to justify their conclusions. If there are actual incidents, perhaps some that have happened within the organization, these will add a sense of reality and urgency to the discussion. Of course, no cases that are under current consideration can be discussed in this way. Material that can be used for training managers to be sensitive to disability issues is mentioned in Chapter 14.

Table 15.1 Controversial scenarios

Incident	Acceptable behaviour	Inappropriate behaviour	Discrimination or harassment
On his 55th birthday an employee is given a walking stick as a joke			
A male employee stares at a female employee when he thinks nobody is watching			
Two females regularly 'rate' each male that enters the room for looks, dress and voice			
Young employees in a small office regularly refer to an older black lady as 'Mammy'			
A man persists in asking another male employee for a date in spite of repeated refusals			
A male manager calls all young women 'darling'			
A male employee always leaps forward to open a door for any female			
An employee sends a sexually explicit joke to another employee by e-mail			
A female manager recruits only women			

In most organizations that examine these issues afresh, a training programme that covers all managers, supervisors and in-house trainers is often required. It will be important for all those concerned to act and speak in a consistent way across the organization. Needless to say, such training should be included in the programme for all those newly appointed to managerial and supervisory posts. If you are concerned about any particular aspect of the law you might find it useful to issue a questionnaire at the end of the training course. This might ask, for example, how it might be applied to some specific examples.

The extent to which your organization will continue this type of training to all levels is a matter you must decide. It is usually helpful to hold, at the very least, short sessions where managers meet with their people to explain the new policies and procedures, and to explore what this might mean in their own particular situation. Again a facilitator can be helpful. If no facilitator can be used, it will be necessary to train the managers to conduct such sessions, normally as part of their own training workshop.

Organizations that need to pay close attention to compliance matters, for example financial institutions and pharmaceutical companies, often have special departments dealing with such issues. In these cases it is wise to consider including compliance with equal opportunity and diversity issues within the responsibilities of that department, and also including equal opportunities and diversity matters within the training courses on compliance.

Positive support

If you institute a change programme that is seen by managers as radical, it will also appear threatening. Managers may fear that failure to conform to the new cultural behaviour might result in disciplinary action or even dismissal. As a matter of fact, in our experience in introducing major change programmes, it is possible that one or two managers may fail to change or may not want to change their behaviour. Such managers must be removed from their management positions. But they should form a very small minority, and any action that is taken should deal sympathetically with managers who find it difficult to operate in a new culture.

> Managers may need support as they seek to embrace diversity

The important factor is to recognize the problem and to provide support for managers, not only in the form of the training mentioned above but also in terms of coaching and co-counselling. Senior managers can take their subordinates aside from time to time and chat to them about incidents that arise and how they should be handled. They may choose to do this when a junior manager is made responsible for the first time for a person of the opposite sex, or a person with a disability, or a person of a different race and culture. The aim is to help managers to cope with these situations in a constructive and positive manner, to recognize the value of diversity and to see these events as opportunities, not threats.

Some people see no distinction between coaching and counselling as very often they are both occurring at the same time, for example when a manager talks with a subordinate about problems in the workplace. However, we see coaching as one person helping another to acquire some of the knowledge, skills and understanding possessed by the first person. Counselling, on the other hand, is when an individual needs help in making decisions that he alone can make. Another person cannot tell him what to do, but they can help by drawing analogies and assisting the individual to develop his thinking around the problem, the factors involved, the alternatives and the likely outcomes.

Thus co-counselling takes place when two managers at the same level talk over their respective problems in turn, and each helps the other to think through the actions that can be taken in specific instances, or in dealing with particular people. In many ways it is better if the managers work in totally different sections, so that manager A is not influenced by her knowledge of the situation in which manager B finds himself. All the data, ideas and decisions therefore come from the manager whose problem is under discussion. We consider co-counselling a valuable means of support for managers facing a culture change. It is a way that managers can use to help each other and to learn from each other.

Progress checklist

? Have you taken the time to ensure that those at the highest levels in your organization are wholly behind the drives to more effective diversity management?

? Assuming that you have aligned your policies, procedures and conditions of service with your policy on diversity, have you set about developing an informal set of behaviours that are consistent with these?

? Do you have plans to ensure that every manager, supervisor and in-house trainer has the training required to understand your policies and procedures, and the insights required to develop appropriate behaviours?

[?] Do your training courses really make managers think about the way they behave?

[?] Is your organization crucially concerned with compliance issues in respect of financial, trading, health or safety matters? Have you considered including diversity and equal opportunity issues within the training to meet compliance requirements?

[?] Have you sought to introduce a positive culture of support for people at all levels, and to encourage managers to share their problems and to learn from each other?

16

Partnership in diversity

Trade unions

In seeking to manage diversity effectively, your organization may well derive considerable benefit from collaborating with other organizations, for example local community groups, special interest groups and voluntary bodies. If the organization recognizes a trade union, the officers could prove to be valuable allies in the move towards the effective management of a diversified workforce. In the United Kingdom, many trade union leaders are keenly interested in the subject and experienced in the methods that can be used.

Major trade unions not only represent the interest of their members, they are also employers. They are in a unique position to see issues of diversity from the employers' and from the employees' position. What they advocate to employers for their members they have an obligation to provide

The Transport and General Workers' Union (T&G) views the management of diversity as a business as well as a moral issue. All sections of the community are potential employees of the union, and also potential members of the union. In other words all sections of the community can be 'customers' and/or employees. In commenting on diversity, the General Secretary, Bill Morris, has said: 'I want the management of the union I lead to look like the people it serves.'

The union has adopted a strategic approach to the development of diversity policies. The strategy requires an agenda which identifies the issues, a structure which ensures the delivery, and a culture which conveys the message. The T&G has a structure of advisory committees which deal with disability and youth. Women and black workers are now represented by mandatory constitutional committees and are, by right, represented on a proportional basis on major committees. There is also a gay and lesbian informal group, and the union supports delegates attending appropriate TUC events.

Although considerable progress has been made, there are still policies to be developed and a culture to be transformed, including stamping out the canteen culture which perpetuates discrimination.

The union's approach is to involve people who suffer discrimination in the formulation of policies designed to eliminate discrimination. Bill Morris is determined to press on with reform and to remain personally responsible for the management of diversity. Although it is vital to lead from the top, the leadership of the union is acutely aware of the need to carry its members when new policies are developed.

Once a new policy has been adopted by the union it is the duty of every member to support it.

for their employees. British trade unions are democratic bodies where the governing bodies and senior executives are elected. Thus, the development of diversity policies is not merely a matter for a few top executives; it is a matter for all the membership to consider.

The insights that responsible trade union leaders can bring to the debate when an employer organization decides to move forward with the management of diversity should not be undervalued. Many trade unions now seek to include diversity issues in their agreements with employers. This should not be seen as any kind of threat, but rather an opportunity to co-operate with responsible trade union leaders in the fight against discrimination. As we have remarked earlier, eliminating discrimination and valuing every individual is not merely a matter for employers and for managers. Every employee is involved, and where an organization recognizes trade unions, the co-operation of the trade union leaders should therefore be welcomed.

Ciro Citterio is a major menswear company with 2000 employees and more than 150 shops in the UK. Under the heading of 'Partnership at Work', Ciro Citterio has entered into a recognition and procedural agreement with the Transport and General Workers' Union covering all its employees. The objectives of this agreement are stated as follows.

'Good industrial relations are a joint responsibility of both parties and need the continuing co-operation of all concerned – management, trade union and individual employees. This Agreement is designed to encourage and assist that co-operation.

'This Agreement provides a system of representation and procedure through which the Parties may raise items of common concern, of either an individual or a collective nature.

'The Parties recognize the importance of ensuring that all management and employee relationships are based on mutual understanding and respect and that employment practices are conducted to the highest possible standards.

'Both Parties are committed to developing equal opportunities and anti-harassment procedures for employees or prospective employees. **Both Parties give a commitment to negotiate a comprehensive equal opportunities agreement after ratification of this Procedural Agreement**. Both Parties are committed to ensure that the treatment of staff will be fair and equitable in all matters of discipline and grievance.'

Employers' organizations, professional bodies and educational institutions

There are a number of employers' organizations and professional bodies that have taken a special interest in these matters. In the United Kingdom and the Republic of Ireland, the Institute of Personnel and Development has taken a leading role in the development of diversity management. Some engineering bodies have taken a special interest in furthering the participation of women in the profession.

A UK organization known as Business in the Community is developing a 'bench mark for diversity'. This body has a wide basis of support from a number of companies and organizations active in the area of bringing together the interests of the community and business. You may find that your own trade organization has taken an interest in this subject and can give you information about how these ideas are being implemented in your industry and by other firms in your sector.

Many colleges and universities have students and staff from a diversity of countries and they often need to confront diversity issues themselves in the way that they operate. Most take both men and women students and have to face the possibility of sexual harassment or discrimination. Many such institutions work closely with local employers and there is often scope for collaboration on diversity issues.

York College, formed in April 1999 by the merger of two major educational institutions, has set about rationalizing its course provision and facilities (including 400 networked computers and 60,000 books and journals). York College offers more than 120 full-time and 400 part-time courses and attracts more than 14,500 students annually. They come from all over the world – from more than 40 countries in recent years – because of its specialist facilities. A number of courses offer the opportunity for exchanges, visits, work placements or internet projects with other European countries.

The college also enjoys excellent links with local employers and community organizations. York College corporate objectives include: 'The College will strive to meet the needs of all students to enable them to progress to their full potential within an inclusive learning environment' and 'The College will work in partnership, as appropriate, to achieve its own objectives and to contribute to the economic and social wellbeing of the wider community.'

Early in the year 2000, York College is in the process of developing its management of diversity policy and already has policies on equal opportunities, harassment and disability that will support this new policy. College policies on recruitment and selection, parental leave, job share and inclusive learning, and also its procedures for dealing with student complaints, will all be closely linked to the management of diversity policy. The college is committed to providing equal opportunities for all students regardless of gender, nationality, ethnic origin, religion or disability, ensuring that appropriate support and advice is available where needed for all students.

By linking with these bodies your organization can gain help and advice about current best practice and learn of case histories of companies which have tackled these issues with varying degrees of success. When these have been well prepared, such case histories can give indications of policies and practices that have been successful – and those that have not. As always, in looking at such data one must take into account the context of the organization concerned, including its geographical location and the extent of the commitment and competence of the senior management team.

Such organizations can give general help and advice and may have valuable information and guidance on specific issues. There are also bodies that provide help on specific topics, and the scope of these types of organizations is outlined below. Because of the number of such bodies you will need to exercise discretion in the extent to which you decide to work closely with them. As a source of information, however, they should not be neglected.

Gender, race and creed

There are a number of responsible women's groups that lobby for the attention of employers and that can provide help and advice to organizations that feel a need to take particular action in this area.

In dealing with gender issues there are also organizations that bring together homosexual men and/or women. These organizations may have a constructive role to play in helping employers to understand the particular problems of these groups, and the measures that can be taken to eliminate discrimination and harassment. They may also be able to give information about how other organizations have tackled some of the particular problems that your organization has to face.

In some areas there are ethnic organizations and clubs and religious communities that bring together particular groups of people who form a significant minority of the local population. If you wish to understand the needs of this group, or to ensure that your message gets across to the members of the group, you will often find the leaders sympathetic. You may well need some patience and understanding in dealing with these leaders if your organization does not have a good record in dealing with them in the past, or a good image in their eyes. You can expect some suspicion and possibly even hostility.

The Cleveland Police Force provides a police service to a population of approximately half a million people in the towns and surrounding areas of Middlesbrough, Stockton-on-Tees, Redcar, Billingham and Hartlepool. The force has actively promoted equal opportunities and diversity policies in a number of ways. Key players in the implementation of the equal opportunities policy include 20 designated equal opportunities officers who are volunteers from all service units. These officers ensure that EO issues remain at the forefront of service unit agendas and deal with local equal opportunity issues. They meet centrally every three months. The force has been conducting Managing Diversity courses since 1997.

The grievance procedure is supported by more than 50 first contact officers, equal opportunities officers, management and the staff associations. First contact officers (FCOs) and equal opportunities officers (EOOs) are trained volunteers from the police and support staff. These officers do not receive additional pay for their advisory work, but they can claim travelling expenses. They provide a confidential listening service, putting the aggrieved person in control by providing advice and guidance and restoring confidence. These officers pursue a formal or informal approach to resolve the problem should the aggrieved person so desire, giving advice and support on the grievance procedures and other options. Ambitious and forward-thinking officers and staff keenly seek these voluntary appointments.

The chief constable directed the establishment of a working party to review the force race relations policy with a view to ensuring that Cleveland Police develop and implement best practice as identified nationally and locally. The working party chaired by a chief superintendent includes representatives from the human resources department, Unison, Police Federation, Middlesbrough racial harassment forum, Racial Equality Council – Cleveland, Commission for Racial Equality – Leeds, the University of Teeside, HQ Community Safety, HQ Training Department and members of staff from ethnic minority groups. Consultations with representatives of ethnic minorities were much improved when a police sergeant who was a member of the same ethnic group became involved in the discussions.

As a result of the Cleveland Police Force's 'Partnership in the Community' initiative, real advances have been made. At the time of writing, about 1.1 per cent of the force is from ethnic minorities compared with 1.9 per cent in the population. The objective is to increase this to 2 per cent (28 officers). 1% of support staff come from ethnic minorities and the aim, again, is to reach 2%. The Commission for Racial Equality has recognized as good practice the application of racial equality standards.

Cleveland Police is a member of the Opportunity Now initiative to promote the role of women in the workplace. Currently one assistant chief constable is a woman. The force has been awarded the Disability Symbol (Two Ticks) as part of the force commitment to meet the requirements of the Disability Discrimination Act 1995.

The answer in most cases is to persevere and to demonstrate your sincerity through deeds, not just words. As in all such dealings, your honesty must be beyond reproach. The problem is that if your organization is interfacing with this community, it is not just yourself or some key representatives – it is virtually everyone who works for you. It is no use stating that your organization will welcome applications for employment from members of a certain group if your policies and procedures prove to be unworkable, or if there is seen to be prejudice on the part of your recruiters. You must not promise what you cannot deliver.

You must make it clear that you are not lowering your standards, but that you very much hope that members of that community have the ability to work effectively for your firm. You cannot go down this road if you have not taken steps (a) to improve the racial tolerance of your managers and workers, and (b) reviewed your recruitment procedures as outlined in Chapter 4.

We have already referred to such questions as religious holidays and how this can be approached. You may need to enquire whether there are any other religious or cultural factors that need to be taken into account in offering jobs to people in the group.

Carers and people with disabilities

In the United Kingdom, organizations concerned with providing support for carers have instigated research that has indicated some of the problems these people face as they seek employment and as they endeavour to maintain their positions. The results of this research to date have been taken into account in the writing of this book, but if you are serious about making provision for such people you should consider keeping in touch with this work.

One of the most significant facts has been that most carers actually want to work, not only for the income that this brings (although this is by no means insignificant), but also so that their lives may be more fulfilled through interests beyond the person receiving care. As a matter of fact, carers who are employed are more likely to be even more effective in their caring role as more 'rounded' people.

By linking up with relevant bodies you may also be able to help carers in your employment to benefit from respite care provision for the person receiving care. Close liaison can help your employed carers to get a proper holiday, and thus return refreshed to their labours.

As we have seen earlier, disability can take many forms. There are constantly significant developments in technology that open up new possibilities for people with disabilities. Specialist bodies dealing with forms of

paralysis, with visual impairment or with those who have hearing difficulties will be aware of these developments as they apply to their members
and those they serve.

Clearing house

In the UK, charitable voluntary bodies exist to help people with most kinds
of needs. Help is often available from public bodies, government departments, local authorities and public health authorities. Whatever problem
one of your employees faces, there is likely to be an organization or
department that can help. Some employers have found it helpful to set up a
database on the organization's intranet so that employees with a problem
can find out where to go to get help. Indeed, we understand that there are
now commercial organizations that will undertake this role for employers
for a fee.

Employees who are committed to your company and who lead busy lives
may find it daunting to find their way through the maze of support available
when they are confronted with a new problem, for example concerned with
caring (such as a newly disabled partner) or with housing or schooling. A
clearing-house service that directs people precisely to the best help available
might prove to be a valuable perquisite, a part of the reward package for
employees.

Community organizations

If you employ a significant number of people in a given geographical area,
it is probably worthwhile to link up with local community organizations.
You may find that supporting such organizations, as appropriate, will
enhance your standing in the community and enhance the environment for
your employees. By linking with these organizations you may be able to
gauge local opinions on matters of concern to your operation and to your
employees.

We have referred elsewhere to the desire of many companies to be
respected in their local communities. By judicious support, for example, of
sporting facilities in the area, you could be helping to provide amenities
from which your employees would derive benefit.

Progress checklist

[?] Does your organization recognize a trade union? Have you been able to establish effective collaboration with this trade union in developing diversity policies and practices?

[?] Does your contact with trade bodies, employer organizations, colleges and universities cover diversity issues?

[?] Are your professional employees involved in organizations that have an interest in diversity? Do they make use of the information and opportunities for collaboration?

[?] Have you identified constructive organizations that serve people with specific needs such as equal rights for women, gays or lesbians or ethnic or religious groups?

[?] Do you have regular information from organizations that help carers or people with specific disabilities?

[?] Have you considered the provision of a clearing house of information that could be used by employees who encounter family or health problems?

[?] Are community organizations relevant to your operation? If so, how do you engage with them?

17

Hot issues

▷ Prepare to be a leader in diversity management in the future

▷ Maintain the initiative in the work-life balance

▷ Be alert to problems arising from racism and religious differences

▷ Secure the business gains into the future from diversity

Take the initiative and keep your finger on the pulse of diversity in your organization. Take full benefit from diversity. While you consolidate your internal programme, keep abreast of some of the issues that are, or that will be important in the near future. Some problems will take years to resolve, yet they are pressing matters that require urgent attention, including further developments in the work-life balance, the inclusion of more carers into the workforce, and the problem of racism in all its forms.

> ▶ Take the initiative and keep your finger on the pulse of diversity

The work-life balance

Modern technology and changes in the pattern of business trading, shopping and leisure have opened up a number of possibilities to enable people to accommodate work and other aspects of their lives. Some of the new patterns of work have been described in Chapters 11 and 12, but here we are concerned with the fact that these changes will continue and employers who wish to retain highly qualified and capable people will need to offer increasingly flexible working hours and reward packages.

There is no doubt that as technology advances, key skilled people will be increasingly difficult to recruit and retain. As we have remarked earlier, all the talent does not reside with prime-age Caucasian males. Companies will need to be seen to welcome people of all types. Already there are signs that very able black graduates are studying potential employers with care to see if their policies towards race are sound. Women graduates will be interested in the potential employer's treatment of ther sex. High flyers in the City of London are very interested in the overall package of benefits offered, as salary alone will not keep them in the firm. Attending to the work-life balance is, therefore, a very real business success issue.

Women who seek to balance their careers with their home and social lives find these problems particularly acute. In most countries this is still a problem. In some areas (notably in Southern England and the American 'Silicon Valley') the problem is compounded by the expectation that people should work long hours, and be prepared to stay at the office late into the evening. Quite often, the work can be completed during the day, but individuals are viewed as keen when working late.

It has been reported that career women in Silicon Valley find it difficult to find suitable men to date. The men are there, but they all work very late hours. The women in question are afraid to use the web as they consider on-line dating risky. 'Who knows who the person really is behind the handle,' wrote one frustrated young woman to *Business Week*. Some are reluctant to meet people through dating agencies, as this would seem to the successful career women an act of desperation.

We are likely to see a reaction to the long-hours syndrome as people react against the disruption to their social and domestic lives. People who look after children, both men and women, are likely to react against a regime that denies them 'quality time' with their offspring.

The fact that the internet operates 24 hours a day every day means that business can be conducted round the clock. People want to shop and deal with their bank accounts at all times of the day and night. These changes in trading patterns can easily spill over into excessive working hours, stress, and damage to family life. There have been calls recently for 'smarter, not longer, working hours', and employers will need to take heed to these calls and to move towards contracts of employment and patterns of work that respect family life.

In many sectors, business requires people to be flexible in the hours they work so as to provide proper cover over the trading periods or manufacturing cycles. At the same time, employees are now requiring business to be flexible in its demands, so that each worker can achieve a satisfying life outside the workplace. This applies to able-bodied people with few commitments as well as to people with disabilities and to those who care for children or for relatives with disabilities or permanently impaired health.

> ▶ **Business requires people to be flexible – and employees expect business to be flexible!**

In March 2000, as part of his proposals to reform the European Commission, Neil Kinnock, Vice-President for Administrative Reform, specifically addressed the management of diversity in a number of ways. In developing new tests for recruitment, account will be taken of the multicultural dimension of the EU as well as of gender, and the Commission also proposes to increase flexibility in retirement age policy. More emphasis will be given to training related to working in a multicultural environment and to managing diversity.

In considering people-friendly policies, consideration will be given to increasing flexibility in working hours, including flexitime, job sharing, part-time working and teleworking. Initiatives to help employees to balance professional lives with family obligations will include parental leave for both parents (including adoption), childcare provision and a right to family leave.

Mr Kinnock sees such reforms as potentially valuable to the work of the Commission, as well as to the advantage of its employees. The Commission proposes to give recognition to stable partnerships outside marriage. It is interesting to note that the Commission responded positively to the results of an extensive consultation exercise with its staff, for example by including reference to empowerment and decentralization in its revised proposals.

The Commission has committed itself to a progressive policy and a 'Code of Good Practice' on the employment of people with disabilities. A bureaucracy employing 16,000 people in many different divisions and locations will not find it easy to implement such far-reaching changes, but clearly the will is there.

Progress has been made over recent years in respect of equal opportunities for women. This has included special training to reduce discrimination, provided for those who set up and conduct recruitment and selection panels. Training has also been provided for women with potential, but here, as in so many areas, there is much more to be done. Like so many large organizations the Commission is not recruiting many staff, and this hinders efforts to redress the balance in respect of gender, race and disability.

Women are still underrepresented in the higher reaches of management. Many explanations have been put forward for this, including the fact that, in general, the management styles of men and women differ markedly. Indeed, it has been said that the only way for a woman to get to the top is to behave like a man. Many women have disproved this narrow view, but generally they have reported that a woman has to work much harder to achieve the same recognition as a man. There are signs, however, that this situation is changing and that 'female' management styles are becoming more recognized as effective. Studies in the USA and the UK indicate that women are more effective in motivational and supportive behaviours, whereas men tend to operate more effectively in the traditional 'command and control' styles. The fact is that the command and control style is becoming outmoded in many situations where every individual's contribution becomes essential for the success of the enterprise.

▶ **Deal with the stress experienced by people at all levels and in all kinds of jobs**

Another explanation of this glass ceiling is the perpetuation of informal organizational cultures that emphasize the traditional male and female roles, cultures that fail to take account of the changing nature of society and of women's ability to manage effectively. Women need to be noticed doing well, as all too often senior management just does not see or recognize their achievements. This is a matter that organizations will need to address.

People at all levels and in all kinds of jobs experience stress. Lone parents and carers have particular problems in coping with stress. Some jobs, especially those dealing with people who are injured, sick or distressed, present their own forms of stress. Organizations will find it increasingly difficult to ignore the stress factor, and many are already providing stress management or stress counselling support for those who are vulnerable.

People want to be more in control of their lives and to develop their potential. Organizations that recognize this and make provision for people to learn and support them in this learning journey will find that this approach has many unexpected benefits. The temptation is to restrict learning support to areas of direct and obvious benefit to the organization. This is not necessary. Once people start to develop their skills and to increase their confidence, their contribution to the firm will also increase – provided they are allowed to contribute through a supportive management culture and style. Support for learning could become a key benefit in the future, and it will be of particular value to those who are currently disadvantaged, and for whatever reason, need to learn more in order to function effectively in our society.

Racism

Unrest due to racism and religious differences is an unwelcome fact of life on the national and international stage. It is not surprising, therefore, to find that it appears in various guises within organizations. Organizations must guard against behaviour and attitudes that can amount to 'institutionalized racism'. Racism consists of words or practices that disadvantage people because of their ethnic origin, colour or culture. When we say that in an organization there is institutionalized racism, we do not mean that every individual, or even the majority of the individuals who work there are racists. We are talking about a development over time, a historical evolution, of policies and practices that amount to a collective failure to demonstrate appropriate and professional respect for people because of their ethnic origin, colour or culture, whether the people concerned are employees or people who interact with the organization.

> ▶ Racist behaviour is often unwitting, unconscious and unintentional

Institutionalized racism can be a particular problem if your organization provides a service directly to individual members of the public – for example a police force, an ambulance service or a local council. In such cases you will wish to monitor public reaction to the services you provide and to pay particular attention to any complaints that you receive. Institutional racism has been reported extensively in the USA and in the UK, but there can be no doubt that it exists in many other countries. Racist behaviour is often unwitting, unconscious and unintentional. In such cases it is not until someone points out the racist nature of words and behaviour that the problem is recognized by the perpetrators.

If you suspect that there is institutionalized racism in any part of your organization, the first thing to do is to seek evidence and the opinions of people who might feel themselves to be the subject of racial discrimination, whether this is in word or deed. There is no point whatsoever in asking an individual if she is a racist. Few people, even the most prejudiced, see themselves as racist. Indeed, many will be affronted by the accusation. One reason for this is that many people who behave in a racist manner actually believe, for example, that all black people have criminal tendencies, that all white people are prejudiced against blacks, or that all French people are untrustworthy.

Such stereotypes are the staple diet of prejudice. What action can be taken to overcome such institutional racism? There are no simple answers. The following actions, if initiated and fully supported by top management, will bring about improvements:

1. Secure top management commitment to eliminating racism.

2. Collect information.

3. Survey perceptions.

4. Provide mediators.

5. Examine key policies (especially recruitment, selection and performance appraisal).

6. Train key people, managers, supervisors, trainers and human resource personnel.

7. Provide awareness training.

8. Actively recruit minorities.

9. Appoint mentors.

10. Keep employees informed.

Advice on these topics is provided in earlier chapters, but some of the points need stronger action if there is institutionalized racism. The most senior management team (the board of directors in a private company) must establish as goals (a) the elimination of racial prejudice and disadvantage, and (b) the demonstration of fairness in all aspects of the organization's dealings with people. The top management team must be wholeheartedly committed to these goals. Without this level of commitment everything else managers do will have little lasting effect. Give senior people the opportunity to develop non-racist ways of thinking and acting through training and coaching. If this fails they must be removed from office.

Introduce and foster a system of co-counselling and co-coaching whereby senior people help each other. A senior person should be able to turn to a trusted colleague and talk through any problems he has with the anti-racist programme. A senior person should be able to take another aside and point out where his words or actions could be interpreted as racist. This kind of community of learning and mutual support can be cascaded down the line. Replacing any negative feature of a culture with positive and constructive features requires constant and consistent effort at every level. But it must start at the top.

Information must be collected about racial incidents, and this collecting process must be maintained. The data must be analyzed by location and by section. People must feel free to report such incidents anonymously without fear of reprisals. However, disciplinary action might be taken against someone if an allegation can be proved to be malicious. Wherever possible, people who leave should have exit interviews with an independent person. From the organization's viewpoint, exit interviews provide an opportunity to learn whether or not racist behaviour plays any part in labour turnover. The information will help top managers to identify areas of the business where racist problems are acute. It will also help the top team to monitor progress – or lack of it.

Surveys will be needed to ascertain the perceptions of the workforce and of the 'customers'. Provide an avenue whereby every employee may report what he perceives to be a racist incident without fear of recrimination. Every such incident should be referred in the first instance to a trained mediator (*see* Chapters 3 and 6). The mediator will seek to resolve the problem without recourse to formal grievance or discipline procedures. If this resolution can be achieved, for example with an apology and a promise that no such incident will be repeated, the incident can be reported anonymously for statistical purposes. If, however, the incident is very serious or if a racist action is repeated, the discipline procedure will need to be used. If the alleged racist action is disputed, it may be necessary for someone in authority to conduct an enquiry simply to establish the facts. Needless to say, the person conducting the enquiry must be considered as impartial by all the parties involved.

Be sure that any training that you 'buy in' shares your policy on equality and racial acceptance. There is no doubt about the fact that awareness training can be an abject failure if (a) it is not conducted in a sensible way, and (b) it is not part of a culture change programme supported by senior management coaching.

The future for diversity

Make sure that the positive gains of your diversity action are clearly identified. This will help to maintain the motivation of senior management. Initiatives of this nature can so easily fizzle out unless the value of the programme is recognized at the highest levels and throughout the organization. Evaluate each initiative, relating achievements to the aims and objectives specified at the outset (Chapter 3).

The equal opportunities adviser of a large bus company, in seeking to implement board policy, wanted information about the number of women, black and disabled people employed at various locations. She sent out a request for this information to the managers at each location. At about the same time, the chief executive wanted information about the number of bus stops in each area and how many of these had shelters attached. After a couple of weeks the response to the EO adviser was scrappy and incomplete, but the chief executive's request was answered in full within a couple of days.

An equal opportunities manager in a large public body sent out a request to the personnel officers in each unit for information about the number of disabled people employed. Few units replied quickly, and some refused to reply at all, stating that this would represent a disclosure of personal information.

Without a firm lead from the top, little can be achieved.

In multinational companies the need for a lead from the people at the centre is vital, but it needs to be taken up by the leaders in each country and at each site if policies on equality and diversity are to succeed. To ensure success into the future:

- recognize explicitly the business case for diversity and emphasize this within the organization. Adhere to legal requirements as a baseline only;
- focus on the positive approach, valuing difference at the individual and group level, rather than considering such differences as problems;
- be prepared to tackle and to manage the culture change required.

SmithKline Beecham (SB) is an Anglo-American company that operates globally, with about 40,000 employees worldwide in 170 countries. The research division has sites in the UK, the USA, Europe, Japan, South Africa and Singapore. The company has a global policy on the management of diversity, and this is managed nationally, taking into account the relevant local labour laws. Developments within the UK and the USA are set within this context.

The SB policy on equality and diversity explicitly recognizes that the company operates in diverse cultures, environments and communities that embrace employees, potential employees, customers, suppliers and shareholders. Thus, SB's aim is to recognize and reflect these differences in its workforce and business environment. The company considers that an innovative and effective equality and diversity policy is an essential factor in achieving world-class competitiveness. The SB definition of equality and diversity is: **'Creating an environment where the potential of the skills and expertise of all our employees are realized through recognizing and valuing differences in people'**.

An example of this international dimension is that the chief operating officer, born in France, reports to the chief executive officer who is of Danish origin. The chairman of the research and development division is originally from Japan.

The policy is implemented through addressing individual and group needs and issues through a flexible and comprehensive set of initiatives. There are clear guidelines for the behaviour of managers, and employees in general. Guidelines have been laid down to cover each step of the employment process, including recruitment and selection, performance assessment, job evaluation, training and development, transfers and promotions, flexible working, harassment and cultural and religious needs. Specific policies and procedures have been developed to deal with harassment and to assist those employees who have disabilities.

Jan Leschly, Chief Executive of SmithKline Beecham, sums up the business case: **'We have to use the abilities of every single individual and utilize their talent. Through proper attention to managing diversity, we will gain sustainable competitive advantage.'**

A change programme is fed by management commitment and by information about progress. If the supply of either dries up, the programme will wither on the vine. Use the intranet, newsletters, briefing groups and team meetings according to the way your organization is run, but keep it up and keep it fresh.

Progress checklist

? How will you keep abreast of developments in this field?

? What steps do you consider your company might have to take in the future to cope with changing work-life demands?

[?] Is the top team ready to meet the challenge of tackling institutional racism? Do you collect information and assess how people see things on the ground? Have you put into place the ten-point action plan?

[?] Have you monitored the progress to date?

[?] Are you looking for future success through managing diversity?

[?] Are you keeping people informed?

Further reading

This list is provided for the senior executive who wishes to delve into the subject more deeply.

Ansari, K.H. and Jackson, J. (1994) *Managing Cultural Diversity at Work*, Kogan Page.

Belbin, R.M. (1999), *Changing the Way We Work*, Heinemann.

Belbin, R.M. (2000) *Beyond the Team*, Butterworth Heinemann.

Edmunds, V., Hopkins, M. and Williams, A. (1998) *Harassment at Work*, Jordan Publishing.

Fenton-O'Creevy, M., Wood, S. and Callerot, E. (1998) *Employee Involvement within European Multinationals: Stage 1 Research Report*, European Works Council Study Group.

Forth, J. and others (1997) *Family Friendly Working Arrangements in Britain in 1996*, Department for Education and Employment/Policy Studies Institute.

Goffee, R. and Jones, G. (1998) *The Character of a Corporation: how your company's culture can make or break your business*, HarperCollins Business.

Handy, C. (1978), *Gods of Management – who they are, how they work and why they will fail*, Pan.

Hofstede, G. (1996) *Cultures and Organization: Software of the Mind*, McGraw Hill.

Institute of Personnel and Development (1999) *The IPD Guide on International Recruitment, Selection and Assessment*, Institute of Personnel and Development.

Johnson, R. (1995) *Perfect Teamwork*, Arrow Business Books.

Johnson, R. and Redmond, D. (1998) *The Art of Empowerment – the profit and pain of employee involvement*, Financial Times Pitman Publishing.

Kandola, R. and Fullerton, J. (1998) *Diversity in Action: managing the mosaic*, Institute of Personnel and Development.

MacPherson of Cluny, Sir W. (1999) *The Stephen Lawrence Inquiry*, The Stationery Office.

Simmons, S. (1996) *Flexible Working: a strategic guide to successful implementation and operation*, Kogan Page.

Thomas, D. (1990) *Alan Sugar: the Amstrad story*, Century.

Trompenaars, F. and Hampden-Turner, C. (1997) *Riding the Waves of Culture – understanding cultural diversity in business*, Nicolas Brealey Publishing.

Index

Bold type is used to indicate where topics are explained or explored.